ANGER MANAGEMENT

A STEP-BY-STEP GUIDE TO OVERCOMING YOUR ANGER & EMOTION

BY RYAN KENT

ANGER MANAGEMENT

© **Copyright 2019 - All rights reserved.**

The content contained within this book may not be reproduced, duplicated or transmitted without direct written permission from the author or the publisher.

Under no circumstances will any blame or legal responsibility be held against the publisher, or author, for any damages, reparation, or monetary loss due to the information contained within this book. Either directly or indirectly.

Legal Notice:

This book is copyright protected. This book is only for personal use. You cannot amend, distribute, sell, use, quote or paraphrase any part, or the content within this book, without the consent of the author or publisher.

Disclaimer Notice:

Please note the information contained within this document is for educational and entertainment purposes only. All effort has been executed to present accurate, up to date, and reliable, complete information. No warranties of any kind are declared or implied. Readers acknowledge that the author is not engaging in the rendering of legal, financial, medical or professional advice. The content within this book has been derived from various sources. Please consult a licensed professional before attempting any techniques outlined in this book.

By reading this document, the reader agrees that under no

circumstances is the author responsible for any losses, direct or indirect, which are incurred as a result of the use of information contained within this document, including, but not limited to, — errors, omissions, or inaccuracies.

TABLE OF CONTENTS

INTRODUCTION V

CHAPTER 1 WHAT CAUSES ANGER? 1

CHAPTER 2 SIGN AND SYMPTOMS OF ANGER PROBLEMS 13

    THE STAGES OF CHANGE IN THE LIFE OF A MAN 17

CHAPTER 3 WHY IS BEING ANGRY VERY UNHEALTHY? 25

CHAPTER 4 HOW TO RELEASE YOUR ANGER WITHOUT VIOLENCE 38

    HOW TO DEAL WITH ANGER AS A SECONDARY 38
        SLOW BREATHING *41*

CHAPTER 5 HOW TO TAKE CONTROL OF YOUR EMOTION AND DEAL WITH ANGER 46

CHAPTER 6 DON'T HOLD GRUDGES 55

    HOW TO LET GO 61
    THE BASIC STEPS FOR LETTING A GRUDGE GO 63

CHAPTER 7 IDENTIFYING WHAT CAUSES YOUR ANGER 69

    ANGER DIARY 71

CHAPTER 8 BE RESPONSIBLE FOR YOUR ANGER 78

    CONSEQUENCES OF BLAMING OTHER PEOPLE FOR HOW WE HANDLE ANGER 82

CHAPTER 9 LONG-TERM AND SHORT-TERM SOLUTION TO ANGER 94

CHAPTER 10 PUTTING IT TOGETHER 103

    THE USE OF ANGER MANAGEMENT TECHNIQUES 103
    PRACTICE MAKES PERFECT 107
    PROGRAMS 108
        ANGER MANAGEMENT CLASSES *110*
        HANDLING A RELAPSE *111*

CONCLUSION 114

INTRODUCTION

Thank you for purchasing *Anger Management: A Step-by-Step Guide to Overcoming Your Anger & Emotion*. Emotions are some of the most pressing issues we have to deal with in our daily lives. Anger is one of the most misunderstood emotion yet it presents in almost all aspects of life. This emotion is very important yet if it is left unmanaged, a lot of damage may occur. Many people find themselves unable to acknowledge or even deal with this powerful emotion. Controlling anger can be a hard and complicated process especially if it has taken deep roots within us, and we are unable to use it constructively.

Purchasing this book is the first step you can take towards managing your anger and becoming better in self-assessment and control. If you have decided to change and live a life free of unnecessary anger and inappropriate expression, this book is designed for you. The first step is always the easiest; however, which is why the information you find in the following chapters is very important to take to heart. The concepts you find herein can be put to action immediately or at a later date depending on your situation.

To that end, this book will cover, the causes of anger, its signs and symptoms and ways to manage it. We have deliberately used the simplest language to explain why uncontrolled anger is unhealthy for you, ways of realizing anger without violence and ways of controlling this emotion. Further, we have defined the connection between grudges and anger, the consequences of holding grudges and ways of letting it go.

This book has also explained how you can identify and monitor your anger triggers, rate your rage and apply techniques to carb it. There is also an explanation of how you can be responsible for your emotions, especially anger, both long term and short-term techniques for anger management.

Thank you once again for purchasing this book. There are many books about anger management on the market, I am glad that you have decided to choose this one! Every effort was made to ensure that this guide is full of useful information. The language used herein is simple so that everyone can get the help he/she needs, please enjoy!

ANGER MANAGEMENT

CHAPTER 1

WHAT CAUSES ANGER?

Anger is a normal and healthy emotion but its power cannot be ignored. This emotion may stem from feelings of hurt, annoyance, frustration, or disappointment. Anger is a normal emotion ranging from mild irritation to destructive rage. Everyone has different anger triggers and what might spark one person may not bother the next person at all. Considering that anger is a normal emotion, we can agree that it has a healthy purpose in our lives. In most cases, it warns us when something is not right. However, anger becomes a problem if it is uncontrollable.

The main challenge with anger is that it seems to come when a person is completely unaware and because it erupts with such ferocity, its intensity can easily overshadow the causes. What most of us gather from being angry or staying with a person who has anger problems is the consequences and damage that it leaves behind. Typically, we cannot remember the cause of the anger in the first place. What is sad is that a person in need of anger management can experience these bouts of intense anger outbursts repeatedly. Such a person may or may not recognize the events that took place leading to anger.

Some of the people suffering from anger issues may feel that they have the right to act out of emotions, therefore, will not feel any remorse for their actions or words. What is even worse for the angry people is that most of them never learn the causes of anger and ways to change behavior and act better thus the cycle will consistently repeat itself.

Primarily, the anger emotion evolved as a means of survival and protection helping people to get away from what is considered wrong. Mild anger may stem from feelings of tiredness, stress or irritability- In fact, we are likely to feel agitated when our basic needs are not met. We may also become angry when reacting to criticism, frustration or threats. In such cases, getting angry is not necessarily an irrational or unreasonable reaction.

We can also get angry or feel irritated by the beliefs, actions, and opinions of other people. Anger tends to affect our ability to communicate in an effective manner thus making us say or do unreasonable things. Being unreasonable or irrational in our moment of anger can make the people around us to feel resentful, threatened, or angry and this will cause more challenges to effective communication and expression.

In other cases, anger arises as a secondary emotion. It can be a reaction to feeling threatened, frightened or lonely. It is very important to understand why you or another angry person is experiencing this emotion so that the real cause can be addressed.

Anger is not simply a state of the mind. His emotion can trigger physical changes such as blood pressure, increased heart rate and release of hormones such as adrenaline which braces one to fight or flight. Due to these physical effects, excessive and uncontrolled anger can be detrimental to the wellbeing of the affected individuals.

If you or a man close to you has a challenge controlling his anger, there is dire need to take steps towards dealing with the emotions in a more constructive way. If high levels of uncontrolled anger are left unsorted, they might lead to relationship problems.

The term anger management is used to describe the skills and techniques that one may use to recognize they are getting angry and take the appropriate actions to handle the situation in an effective way. Note that, anger management does not mean suppressing or internalizing anger. Although anger can be considered healthy, suppressing and internalizing it can lead to more harm than good.

Some of the dangers of suppressing anger include depression and anxiety. When one is unable to express anger in an appropriate way, he or she may experience mental problems including withdrawal, unwarranted tension, overreacting to a situation, among others. Suppressed anger can disrupt relationships, affect behavioral patterns and effective thinking and also create a variety of physical problems. Suppressed anger has been linked to problems such as emotional and physical abuse, crime and other violent behavior.

Anger management involves recognizing the triggers of the emotion as early as possible and dealing with them (expressing them) in a calm cool and collected way. Basically, we learn how to deal with strong emotions as we grow up. Chances are, if we saw someone close to us expressing their anger in a wrong way, we might think it is a good and effective way, thus follow it unconsciously. Anger management is about unlearning these ineffective coping mechanisms and learning more constructive ways of dealing with the frustration and problems associated with anger.

The frequent challenges in our day to day lives as men can lead us to tough feelings of anger. This emotion can stem from a variety of experiences such as annoyance, frustration, hurt and disappointment. Some men use anger as a defense mechanism, their only weapon when they feel powerless. This mechanism may develop as a result of traumatic experiences as a child such as shaming, danger or abuse. Under such a situation, telling a man to get a hold of his anger might lead to strong resistance because, for him, it would sound like a challenge to lower his defense mechanism. Basically, anger in men is usually a go-to response used to cover other underlying emotions such as stress, grieve, frustration or dissatisfaction.

Anger management is one of the important ways that a man may apply to address the underlying issues they might be facing. Additionally, proper anger management can help one to avoid disrupting relationships. Again, anger management will ensure that a person keeps a leveled head during challenging situations and makes better decisions.

In one of the anger management boot camps held by Dr. Steven Stosny, most of the men undergoing the therapy sessions rated themselves worthy of love but most of them felt that the love they gave was insufficient. Simply put, these men overestimated their need for love yet underestimated the importance of their love to their loved ones.

On the surface, the tension between feeling lovable and being unable to meet the emotional needs of the loved ones can make a man seem entitled – more like he expects to be loved without giving anything in return. However, on a deeper level, This tension also explains why a large number of men hold are emotionally withheld in their relationships.

Basically, if a person thinks that his love is a da Vinci painting, he will feel the need to share it with other people. On the other hand, if a man feels that his love is like an old sock, he will not bother his loved ones with it. Instead, he will try to compensate for the perceived love deficiencies with some form of service or financial support. In the event that the loved ones or family show that these compensation methods are not adequate, then the man is likely to get angry or resentful.

Most of the anger in men comes from feelings of inadequacy, especially as a provider, protector or lover. These vulnerabilities can acutely be stimulated by mear displeasure or unhappiness of loved ones such as the wife even if their negative state or distress has nothing to do with the man. Once the man sees himself as inadequate and assumes that the wife is displeased about it, he will see himself as the victim. The undeserved blame and victimhood give the man a temporary sense of righteousness, combined with the impulse to retaliate, which in turn triggers anger.

The adrenalin rush resulting from anger, similar to any other amphetamine effect, leads to some level of depression at least in the form of energy depletion and self-doubt. To get out of the depressed state, the man will use a low-grade resentment to gain some temporal form of energy and confidence. The resentment will keep the man partially aroused and also highly susceptible to anger outbursts for long periods of time. The excessive levels of cortisol and adrenaline in his blood make it hard to rest or sleep well and even make it more challenging to concentrate while awake. The state of anger leads to feelings of distraction and tiredness, and the affected person will need more anger to help generate energy, motivation, and focus.

This cycle of getting angry in order to get energy continues and the man finds himself stuck in a roller-coaster of resentment, - anger - depression. The chronic self-blame keeps him stuck in the victim identity which continuously sparks the anger cycle. If this man allows himself to feel like the victimizer, he might get more depressed and even sink to thoughts of suicide.

Once this anger pattern becomes a habit, the reason for getting angry is no longer important. All that the angry man cares about is every opportunity that will anger him and cause the adrenaline rush he needs. Consequently, the man becomes an anger junkie, looking for every opportunity to take the blame and get his hormonal fix. He will be living in two predominant emotional states 1) mildly depressed mood or 2) some form of unexplained anger. His life becomes a lacking drive to get things done and moving on to tomorrow.

When a man feels that his love is inadequate for his loved ones, he does not need insights about the past to feel bad. This anger cycle has nothing to do with childhood trauma; rather, it is about his feeling inadequate for his family today. True, his childhood experiences might have caused the feelings of anger in the first place but the current pattern is arising from constantly blaming the people closest to him. The current habit makes him feel more vulnerable and causes untold misery to his loved ones. Once a habit is instilled in the brain, it cannot be undone by resolving the issue that caused the problem in the first place. That is why the therapies focusing on childhood wounds might not work for such a person because they will hardly change the habits developed in adulthood. The resentment anger depression cycle can only be reconditioned in the present.

A man needs to learn that inadequacy is not a punishment; rather, it is a motivation that should make one want to become better. Our culture has taught us to be as perfect as can be even in our first attempt of anything without realizing that we have to learn things before getting them right. Inadequacy is the fuel driving us to better performances. The unpleasant feeling should force us to learn how to perform the task at hand. That includes maintaining relationships in this complex world.

To become successful in the current complex world, you must develop the habit of picking motivation from the feeling of inadequacy. These feelings should drive one to improve his relationships and life at large. You should realize that these bad feelings are not met to put one down; rather, they call upon him to be more loving and protective. By developing positive habits such as connecting by protecting, the man will realize that he feels more powerful and valuable when compassionate than when defensive and angry.

Like all emotions, anger is trying to tell you something. Basically, it feels us that something is wrong. It is important to note that what is wrong is not necessarily the cause of your anger. It could be something deeper, from the far past, in fact, you might have forgotten about it. Therefore, we should not ignore the message from the anger get so distracted with stopping it that we miss fixing its triggers.

A large number of men attend anger management sessions because they are told by their partners. In most cases, a man with anger issues is told "Go and have your anger issues fixed" yet the causes of the anger are ignored. What we often ignore or overlook is the source/cause of the anger issues in a man.

Men struggling with anger issues need to understand the causes and consequences of their problem in order to effectively take responsibility for their emotions. As easy as it might sound, taking responsibility for one's anger can be very challenging. Basically, anger in men is mostly a reaction to external circumstances. As such, it can be difficult for a person to manage emotions they are linking to external things and other people. However, being angered or provoked is not a valid reason to become abusive, or overactive to the people around you. Unfortunately, any uncontrolled anger issues can lead to abusive and violent behavior, especially in men.

As a man assesses and deals with his anger management issues, the people around him, including partners should be willing to look at their contributions to the problem. In many cases, partners know the things they do that trigger anger in the man they care about but do nothing to change and handle things in a different way. It is important for everyone to acknowledge their contributions and role in anger management especially in a relationship (Spouses). Of course, the causes and triggers of anger need to be assessed from a reasonable point. If you become angry everymen a person clangs a bowl with their spoon while eating, it does not mean that everyone should stop eating.

ANGER MANAGEMENT

One of the common complaints received from men as they undergo anger management sessions is that their spouse/partner is very 'nagging'. Nagging does not only fuel anger in a relationship but also may make a person to lose interest in the partner. Most men find nagging a real turn off. However, that should not be a reason for losing tempers and acting out violently. Unfortunately, many relationships lack honest communication thus the partners have no platform to share important information. Consequently, the nagging continues as each person tries to express him/herself indirectly and the anger escalates. Here, every person in the relationship has a responsibility. If your partner complains because you leave your socks on the floor, pick them up and learn to store them appropriately.

Communication will help partners to understand each other better and evaluate the causes of nagging and anger. Most nagging wives will justify their behavior by saying that the husband has to be reminded over and over again to have certain things done. On the other hand, the man will say that he is angry because the wife keeps repeating things.

One of the main challenges in anger management for men is that the issues and consequences are normally a cover for the real problem. For instance, the man might get angry instead of expressing the fact that he hates being nagged. Instead of telling the wife/spouse about his feelings for a particular situation, the man will act out and solve nothing. If your anger as a man acts like a hair trigger, Chances are, there are some deeper issues affecting you that need to be addressed. Basically, if a person harbors problems and fails to deal with them in time, they will take up mental space and energy. As a result, the person will not be able to keep things in perspective and the ability to react proportionately to situations is limited.

When dealing with nagging and the communication-related issues that cause anger in men, it is important to identify for effective communication techniques to pass information. First, fix the reason for the nagging in the first place. For instance, as a man, keep your promises, and hold your end of the bargain in the house. Obviously, nagging is not the only cause of anger problems in men regardless of the causes, we need to dig deep enough and get the true trigger of the anger.

CHAPTER 2

SIGN AND SYMPTOMS OF ANGER PROBLEMS

We all experience the emotion of anger, whether it is towards another person, situation or something. One may even feel angry due to the injustices taking place in the world. However, there is a difference between occasional anger and having anger issues. For many people who have anger going beyond the occasional occurrences, there are some signs that might indicate anger management issues.

Regardless of the consequences arising from anger such as interpersonal conflicts, family problems, and difficulties in marriages, criminal activities, imprisonment and outbursts at work, this emotion is very powerful. It can get out of control in the least expected ways. Being able to identify the signs of anger can help a person to think clearly and solve issues effectively.

The best place to look for indicators that you have issues with managing anger is with the loved ones closest to you. Most of us can do a very good job of hiding our anger issues, either consciously or subconsciously, from our friends and coworkers. However, it can be hard to hide from our partners, spouses, and close family members because they get a chance to see us when we are at our most genuine state. We tend to feel safe around our loved ones and unfortunately, we are more likely to take out our anger on them. For some of us, the anger problem leads to difficulties in our relationships, jobs, and families.

What can anger look like to the people around us? According to most partners living with men with anger issues, life can be very scary. In fact, some of them say that the anger appears like a Great White Shark – very fearful. If a person is struggling with anger issues, there will be indicators. Some of the real-life examples of anger indicators mentioned by people living with friends and loved ones who are struggling with anger include:

1. Asking him questions will only get him angry
2. Once he is angry, the name calling starts
3. How can I communicate with him without getting him really angry?
4. Before the incident happened, I had seen the signs of temper and anger.
5. I hate the fact that anger interrupts our conversations. I do not even get the chance to open up.

Do you recognize yourself or someone with anger issues in the above statements? If so, you (or the other person) might be having anger issues. There are various indicators of anger management problems and some of the most common in men include;

Lack of patience,

ANGER MANAGEMENT

Short temper and irritability,
Shutting down and withdrawal,
Belittling, criticizing, and putting others down,
People around you are afraid, - like they are walking on eggshells around you

1. Disproportionate anger

One major sign of anger management issues is when a person reacts to a situation with a greater deal of anger than most people would under similar circumstances. For instance, a person who becomes very angry just because he could not find his favorite beer at the store might be suffering from anger management problems. Disproportionate anger is more than the occasional snappiness or bad mood.

2. Anger without cause

If you or a person you know complains of feeling angry even without a specific cause, then it might indicate anger management challenges. Normal and healthy anger only arises as a response to an upsetting situation. Any anger arising for no particular or valid reason is an indicator of an underlying problem.

3. Intense memory-related anger

If you are getting extremely angry about events and incidents that occurred in the far past, it might indicate anger management problems. The fact that events from the pats can continue to have a strong hold on you or another person and lead to intense angry indicates that one is unable to let go. This might indicate that the person has deep anger management problems.

4. Guarded interactions

If you observe that people are guarded and even cautious when talking to you most of the time, then you might be having anger management problems. If they talk to you as if they are afraid that a time bomb might explode, then you might be in need of anger management help. You may observe that other people are avoiding confrontations or questions so as not to get on your nerves. If you also have people breaking off contact with you or trying to avoid you. That might be an indicator of anger management issues where they feel intimidated when having a conversation with you.

5. Being confronted by others

If some people have actually faced you and mentioned that you have issues with anger management, then it might be a clear indicator that you need help. One or two people might be wrong about you needing anger management help but if the topic keeps coming up from several people, then it is a good idea to reevaluate yourself

Though anger is a normal emotion felt by all human beings, the way we choose to express it may be unacceptable and abnormal to the people around you. If you realize that you have an anger problem, it is important to identify ways of gaining better control over this emotion. Anger management can be achieved through self-help groups and books or in therapy programs. Normally, help for anger management is available online, in workplaces through employee assistance programs, through local counseling clinics among others. Anger management programs are set to help a person to learn ways of controlling anger in order to improve health prospectus and relationships. In due course, you can gain mastery of the anger problem. However, any change of character can only be effective to the extent you allow.

In most cases, learning to control anger is an ongoing task and one will have to rethink the automatic responses. Anger management also helps a person to take more responsibility for his/her thoughts and actions more than he/she did in the past. Al that is required is a plan and a lot of discipline. Having a perspective of what normal anger and anger management looks like will give you an idea of the direction to head towards.

The stages of change in the life of a man

Men tend to go through a set of stages that can be correctly predicted. The progress through these stages is normally a result of technique, motivation, and dedication. While some men move through the stages very first, others take a long while. In fact, some will take a step or two back before moving forward.

As you look at the stages of change listed below, try to assess how each one affected and led to the current state of your life. Also, imagine how you will get past the challenges of every stage as you reach for your anger management goals. Note that your life and experiences may not mirror the order listed below in each detail but understanding them will map a way to your goals.

Point to note:

Choosing to take control of our anger represents a big part of your life and such a change will define how you live your life from this moment onwards. Most men do not make the decision to make big changes in life unless something comes along and motivates them to clear and apply new and better ways of living. Changes normally require self-examination and assessment of new ways of doing things. A large number of people only decide to manage their anger after a serious social, personal or occupational consequences have occurred due to lack of control. The need to manage anger can occur after one has started a divorce process, gotten into a fight or yelled back at the boss in a workplace. Some men will feel the need to manage anger even without being pushed by other people while others will require someone to consistently force them.

The stages of change are:

1. Awareness - A man becomes aware of his problem and looks for its definition. What does it involve and how has it affected my life? In anger management, This stage normally begins when the affected person starts to seek information about anger and its management. HE will look for the definition of

anger, its components and its effects on relationships and health. Finally, how can this anger be controlled?

2. Preparation - The first stage, awareness, only involves the gathering of information. There is no commitment whatsoever. However, the preparation stage involves decision making and actual efforts towards making a change. How will you be expressing anger from this point henceforth? Beyond committing to change, the preparation stage involves self-analysis and planning. It is therefore important to keep an anger management journal where you record the things triggering your anger, the effects, and the consequences. This anger management journal will help you to identify and understand your anger patterns. It will also give you some inside information on how proportional your anger reactions are to the different situations provoking them. The more you understand your anger, the higher your chances of success in changing how you express your emotions.

3. Action – In this third stage, a man starts to make real changes. You may choose to take a self-help course or go for professional therapy sessions depending on the information you gather in the two previous stages. Any approach you choose should enable you to have a better grip on your anger. However, these anger management plans will only work if you apply them with persistence and dedication.

4. Maintaining gains - This final stage does not have an end. It is a continuous phase. This is the stage mostly teaching people about their imperfections. You are human and are bound to make mistakes. Sometimes you will act inappropriately even when you are very well prepared for the worst. On the brighter side, you learn that you can recover from the lapses whenever they occur. Reaching a stable level of sustained behavior takes time and involves a tough process full of dedication and patience. You might go through multiple failures before gaining full success. each time you face a relapse, use the tools and techniques gathered along the way to recover and retry.

It is quite difficult for people with anger management problems to work up a strong enough motivation to want to get through an anger management program. This is because anger has a self-justifying and seductive quality to it and a person will not want to let that go. Most men need to suffer serious anger consequences before they take the necessary steps. Even after starting the program, most angry men will drop off along the way. Some of those who finish the programs stop applying the learned techniques as soon as the practice period is over. Others keep repeating the program until they benefit. Among all these attempts to control anger, you need to know that success can only be achieved with consistency and perseverance. There is no shortcut to controlling your anger.

Before learning the techniques for managing your anger, you need to learn how to recognize your emotions. Learning the exact signs of your anger will take some time and self-analysis. There are different signs of anger classifiable in two, physical, and emotional.

Some of the physical indicators of anger include headaches,

- Clenched jaws, Grinding teeth, Stomachache,
- Sweating, Increased heart rate,
- Feeling hot in the face and neck, Dizziness, shaking and trembling
- Some of the emotional indicators of anger include
- Irritability, resentfulness, Guilt, depression, and sadness,
- Verbal and physical lashing out
- Anxiety, the need to get away from a particular situation
- In some cases, one might notice that he is
- Pacing, rubbing he head,
- Raising his voice,
- Cupping one fist on the other hand
- Getting sarcastic, Losing his sense of humor,
- Crying, yelling or screaming
- Acting in an abusive way or abrasive manner
- Craving for a smoke, drink or other substances that help him relax

These signs and symptoms normally determined by the level of anger. For instance, at very intense levels of anger, a person might sweat, get increased heart rate, become abusive, and choose to abuse drugs. At lower levels of anger, a person might only feel sweaty, pace a bit, get irritated but not reach the extents of becoming violent.

You need to understand how your anger manifests itself under different circumstances. You may have to get into the habit of measuring your own anger in order to get a better glance of your behavior. Unlike body temperature or heartbeat rate which is a physical state thus can be measured using tangible instruments, anger is a complex feeling. It involves emotional, physiological and psychological aspects. Body temperature can be measured using a calibrated thermometer and in order to track anger, it is important to make anger ratings.

Imagine a thermometer that records the amount of anger you are experiencing at any given time. Imagine that every time you are slightly frustrated, upset or irritated, the mercury found in the bulb of a thermometer begins to rise. When the slight irritation begins to turn into anger but you can still control it, then the mercury rises halfway in the thermometer tube. When your anger is literally boiling and you are completely upset, imagine the mercury rising all the way up to the highest calibrations of the thermometer. Rate your anger from 0 to 100 on that thermometer. In this case, 0 means you are completely calm while 100 means that you are completely enraged.

Use the anger thermometer to rate your anger. For a start, think of a recent situation that got you very upset. How angry were you during that moment? Rate that anger on the thermometer. Identify another situation and repeat the process. Chances are, you will notice some similarities with the rate of anger experienced under certain circumstances.

The goal of anger rating to help you recognize that anger runs on a continuum meaning that it moves up and down between calmness and complete rage. People with anger issues do not get their anger ratings on a continuum basis. Their anger curve is not smooth; rather, it fluctuates between fine and furious. At one moment, things may seem completely fine and then suddenly they move to furious.

Even though a person with anger management issues appears to be tuned to "On and off" anger, one can still identify a curve. An angry person might miss all the other anger episodes because he concentrated only on those that are way up and throws the rest in the 'fine' category. With practice, such a person can learn how to spot other shades of anger and peace.

Anger rating is essential because they give us feedback about how likely we are to explode with anger under particular situations and the intensity of our emotions. These ratings can be used to help us recognize when we are getting increasingly upset but are not yet entirely angry, and to improve our chances of being able to stay in control by taking the necessary steps to reverse the rising trend of anger.

CHAPTER 3

WHY IS BEING ANGRY VERY UNHEALTHY?

The thing about anger – it is often very clear cut. Anger is not an emotion you can hide for all your life. At one point, uncontrolled anger will affect you. We ask- is there an emotion that is more misunderstood than anger? Many people believe that holding in this emotion is bad for you – it only builds on the pressure to express and the moment it chooses to come out, it will do so in unexpected ways. Prolonged anger and sudden busts are unhealthy for you. This emotion is very strong and it tends to arouse the nervous system. In fact, it produces effects in the entire body. Sadly, anger eats away at your vital organs, more so the cardiovascular system. It affects your gut and hijacks the nervous system. It also affects your ability to think clearly. Besides, unattended anger tends to grow within the body.

Just because the suppression of anger is bad does not mean that all forms of expression are good. You are not necessarily better off through expression – You might destroy the things and people around you. Anger does not always go away just because a person has unleashed it –

No. Expressing anger does not always offer a catharsis. Furthermore, venting anger, either in words or actions does not make it easier to manage. Often, inappropriate venting only increases the intensity of our feelings. Anger can be classified as self-sufficient – it feeds on itself and multiplies. Plus, when we use aggression to express anger, we bring irreversible damage to ourselves and the people around us.

Majority of us have a challenge managing anger and other intense negative emotions. Interestingly, anger is one of the emotions that men consider 'acceptable' to display. The society has taught men that it is wrong to show weakness and every challenging issue can be solved through violence. Bottom line, a man should not accept defeat easily. More interesting, the men do not always take anger well when someone else is displaying it towards them.

Though men are allowed by society to display their anger, women are not. In most cultures, women are forced to conceal their anger. In fact, they become so good at hiding their anger; it becomes a natural part of them. Simply because anger is so forceful and negative when expressed irrationally, many people fear it, therefore, creating taboos on the open display of anger. Maybe you can recall a time during your childhood when someone (could be you or another person) tries to express their anger by stomping around the house Then someone commanded them to stop being childish.

Maybe you can remember someone who tried to share his/her anger feelings with mom and instead, he/she got canned. The sad fact is, under such unfavorable conditions, no one learns how to express or manage anger appropriately. All we learn is how to hide, suppress or ignore anger, and in extreme cases, we throw it out on another person. This is the same stage where we learn to blame someone else for our feelings.

Studies have revealed that if a person is able to identify and label emotions in a correct way, and also talk about them in a straight forward manner to the point of feeling understood; it is easier for him/her to make negative feelings dissipate. Consequently, the psychological arouse that occur from such feelings also disappear dramatically.

However, when the society is unable to look at anger constructively thus deeming it totally unacceptable, people stay in a state of emotional arousal because they cannot label what they are feeling as anger. We become unable to pay attention to the things going on around us. Further, we are unable to constructively express anger.

The denial makes us unable to understand and regulate our behavior because we stay focused on the inner emotional state. In fact, we tend to experience excessive physical arousal in situations where negative emotions are involved. However, because of the taboos, we do not show any external signs of anger or negative emotional response. Imagine how confusing that is for a friend or spouse. It is also confusing for us.

In some cases, however, we experience feelings of relief after opening up and sharing with someone about our anger and its cause. Psychologists say that this kind of intense relief is experienced because, instead of venting OR expressing ourselves in an unconstructive way, we acknowledge the circumstances leading to our emotional state and constructively work towards finding a solution.

And that positivity points towards the benefits of anger. It acts as a motivator for us to change. Anger encourages us to speak about the things bothering us and find solutions.

But the good and bad of anger is all in how we express ourselves. As anger is pushing us to action about the upsetting things, it also drives us to overreact. The first thing we should ensure is that we lengthen our anger fuse – we do not have to react to every little upsetting thing - instead, we can think our way to a viable solution.

Some of the ways you can use to lengthen your anger fuse include;

- Take three deep breaths.

On the most basic level, anger builds up tension in the body. Breathing deeply in and exhaling will help to ease the tension and consequently lower your anger.

- Change your environment

ANGER MANAGEMENT

Anger can be a trap and the longer you stay in a situation that is upsetting you, the more likely you are to act out irrationally. So, the quickest and most effective way of uncoupling yourself from the ongoing source of anger is to walk away. At least take a five-minute break from the scene and get some fresh air. If you are stuck in traffic, make a mental escape by singing at the top of your lungs or turning up the radio.

- Know the cause of your anger.

Using the anger diary, track down the events, things, and people that trigger anger. Normally, anger is a mask for our deepest fears. Therefore, look beyond the surface – what deep and hidden fears are making you angry right now.

- Let go of what you cannot control.

As you look for ways to manage your anger, know that the only thing you are actually capable of changing is yourself. It is not upon you to control how other people act, but how you react to them is entirely your choice. Getting angry does not fix the situation and in fact, it will make you feel worse. If someone keeps triggering your anger, walk away from them. If walking away is not a plausible solution, brainstorm for other possibilities.

- Express your feelings

As you share how you feel, be sure to use measured tones and think first. Use the right words which are not emotionally loaded. Ensure that you are communicating in a non-confrontational but firm way. State that you are angry, explain your reason and try to find a solution.

- Be cautious

Expressing how you feel in a constructive and appropriate way is a good thing. However, you need to look out for dangerous situations. For instance, if you have a jealous or abusive partner, avoid sharing with him/her. Instead, vent t a friend or trusted person. You might find a solution to your problem in a way you never imagined.

- Be assertive in expressing your feelings and avoid aggression

Assertiveness requires you to speak in a nonviolent yet effective way. Sometimes you may have to rehearse your answer before delivering it to the other person.

- Make positive statements

You may have to internalize some positive statements which you chant to yourself when angry. These statements will serve as a reminder that you are responsible for your own behavior. Saying the statements to yourself will also buy you some time to think before acting. They protect you from knee jerk reactions. For instance, you can say- "I can take care of my needs." "The needs of other people are as important as mine." "I am capable of making good choices."

Regardless of whether you express or suppress anger, this emotion can make you ill.

Uncontrolled anger is an emotion that has adverse physical effects. When we are angry, our bodies normally release cortisol and adrenaline hormones. These are the same hormones released when we undergo stress. When these hormones are released, our pulse, blood pressure, breathing rates, and body temperature may increase, and in extreme cases, to potentially dangerous levels. The chemical and hormonal reactions taking place when we are stressed are designed to give us instant power and a boost of energy to enable the fight or flight mode. This means that the mind and body are activated to run or defend themselves from danger.

However, people with anger management issues (getting angry often) can become ill because of the unregulated physical reactions. Just like stress left unmanaged, anger too can make a person ill. Basically, our bodies do not have the capacity to handle excessive levels of cortisol and adrenaline especially if these hormones and chemicals are constantly released. Some of the problems that may occur because of regular anger occurring over long periods of time include;

- Sleep problems
- Skin disorders
- Problems with digestion,
- Aches and pains more so in the back and head,
- The reduced threshold of pain,

- High blood pressure which might lead to cardiac arrest and stroke
- Impaired immunity,
- Anger may also lead to psychological problems including;
- Depression
- Alcoholism
- Self-injury
- Substance abuse
- Eating disorders
- Reduced self-confidence

Some of the key things you should note about anger being unhealthy for you are;

- Chronic anger will increase your chances of getting a stroke or heart attack. It will also weaken your immune system.
- The best ways to deal with anger immediately include taking deep breaths and walking away.
- In the long term, anger can be managed through identifying its triggers, changing your reactions and seeking professional help.

Anger can be good when expressed in a healthy way and addressed quickly. In fact, under certain circumstances, anger can help one to think rationally. However, unhealthy anger will wreak havoc within your body and also to the people around you. When you hold anger in for long periods, it will explode into a full rage. If y have unhealthy episodes of anger or are prone to losing your anger every so often, below are some of the reasons you should learn anger management.

- Anger outbursts put your heart at risk.

Researches have revealed that anger outbursts affect a person's cardiac health. How so? Basically, in the first two hours after an outburst, your chances of getting a heart attack double. This research was found to be truer in men. Anger is physically damaging.

If you fail to express anger in an appropriate manner, it becomes some quiet poison in the body. Gradually, repressed anger will explode and might lead you to an early death. Researchers found that people who are more prone to anger (and that anger becomes part of their personality) are at a higher risk of coronary disease compared to those who are less angry.

To protect your ticker (heart), it is important to identify and address your emotions and more so anger before they go out of control. Basically, everything in excess is poisonous. However, it is important to note that constructive anger is not associated with heart diseases.

Constructive anger involves that which you speak directly to the person that is upsetting you and identifying a solution. It is the kind of anger that makes you more rational.

- Anger increases your chances of getting a stroke.

ANGER MANAGEMENT

If you have a challenge of controlling anger and you keep lashing out at people for every other thing, beware. One study revealed that people with anger management challenges are at three times higher risk of getting a stroke. How? you may ask. During the two hours following an anger outburst, there are chances of getting a blood clot in your brain and bleeding within the brain to death. For those with an aneurysm in one or more of the brain arteries, there is a six times higher chance of rupturing it after an outburst.

The good news is that one can learn how to control these explosions. First, identify your triggers, then learn how to change your responses. Instead of letting your anger control you, do some exercises, change your environment, use assertive communication skills, learn some other anger management skills to stay in charge.

- Anger weakens your immune system

If you are angry all the time, you might have noticed that you get ill often. The confused state of your body that occurs when you are angry interferes with the levels of the antibody immunoglobulin A. These are the body cells' first line of defense against illnesses and anger issues lower them for at least six hours after an outburst. If you are habitually angry and keep losing control, protect your immune system through several coping strategies including effective problem solving, assertive communication, through restructuring and humor. You need to get away from the black and white mentality and be more open to the opinions of others. Remember that agreeing with the opinion of another person does not make you a loose. Letting another person have his/her way does not make you weak. Either way, you have to start staying calm for the sake of your immunity.

- Anger problems make a person anxious.

Lack of control makes you worried though you may not notice. Anger and anxiety go hand in hand. One study conducted in 2012 revealed that anger can worsen the symptoms of generalized anxiety disorder. This condition is characterized by uncontrollable and excessive worry that interrupts the normal life of a person. People with GAD were found to have higher levels of anger and also hostility. This anger was mostly internalized and unexpressed thus contributing more to the severity of the anxiety problem.

- Anger has also been linked to depression.

Anger, Aggression, and depression are connected. According to numerous studies, these three states are interconnected especially in men. Most people suffering from depression have passive anger – that is, a form of anger whereby a person ruminates about the issue at hand but hardly takes action. The biggest problem with this kind of anger is that it pulls the person deeper into the cycle of depression. Psychologists advise that when one is struggling with depression, he should get busy in order to avoid over-thinking about things.

Any activity that gets your mind off the things brewing anger is advised. Get involved in biking, golfing, painting, singing, or any other thing that draws your mind away from anger. These activities tend to fill your mind up and draw it to the present moment. There is no more room for you to brew anger once your mind is occupied by other things.

- Anger can hurt your lungs.

If you thought that smoking is the only bad practice that might hurt your lungs, here is some news. Being perpetually angry can hurt your lungs. Anger leads to hostility which in turn affects the capacity of your lungs. A research conducted by Harvard University scientists over eight years about anger and its effects found that people with chronic anger and high hostility rates had a lower lung capacity compared to others. The men with the highest hostility rating had a lower lung capacity. Consequently, they were at risk of developing some respiratory problems. The scientists theorized that an increase in stress hormones associated with feelings of anger creates inflammations in the airways.

- Anger shortens life.

As the saying goes, happy people live longer. Stress is directly connected to general health. Stress and anger interfere with your lifespan. A research conducted by the University of Michigan revealed that people who held onto anger for long have a shorter lifespan than those who express their feelings in a constructive way.

ANGER MANAGEMENT

If you are a person who is uncomfortable expressing his emotions, practice how to constructively share your feelings. If working on your own does not seem to work, seek help from a therapist. A healthy expression of anger is actually very beneficial. If a person infringes on your rights you have every reason to tell them that they are wrong. Ensure that you tell people exactly how you feel and what you need in a firm yet respectful way.

CHAPTER 4

HOW TO RELEASE YOUR ANGER WITHOUT VIOLENCE

How to deal with anger as a secondary

In most cases, anger is a secondary emotion meaning that another emotion can be found underneath such fear or sadness. Worry and anxiety can lead to fear while experiences of loss discouragement and disappointment can lead to sadness. The feelings of fear and sadness will make us feel vulnerable, uncomfortable and not in control. And because we are afraid of feeling vulnerable and at a loss, we opt for anger and acting out in an attempt to feel strong. Usually, we shift to this anger node unconsciously. As opposed to fear and sadness, anger gives us a surge of energy, making us feel powerful and in control rather than helpless and vulnerable. Essentially, anger can be a substantial way of creating a sense of power and control in the face of uncertainty and vulnerability.

To illustrate anger as a cover-up emotion, let us look at an example. A couple is yelling at each other because they are angry. However, when you assess the situation again, you will realize that one of the spouses or both of them are trying to hide their fear of abandonment under the anger. In this instance, the combination of anticipation and fear fuels anger. In other cases, uncertainty can trigger anger for instance when you do not have adequate information on a particular topic and things feel amorphous. Why? Because uncertainty and lack of information are linked to the 'unknown' which is actually scary for most people. Boredom has also been linked to anger or irritability as some people feel like they are unproductive and are a loss.

Though having a 'sense of control' is associated with greater wellbeing (especially emotional), excessive desire to stay in control can lead to misery and suffering because it is impossible to stay in charge at all moments of life.

So, when you feel angry or out of control, be it mild or strong, pause and try to identify the main emotion that is driving your anger. During the moment of anger, it can be hard to note the cause of the emotion, therefore, when your feelings calm down, start by exploring your thoughts. Are they the cause of your anger? In most cases, it is our perceptions and thoughts that drive anger. Note that the shift from a basic emotion such as sadness or fear to anger can be very fast and unconscious – in fact, you might miss it. Feelings of anger can be so deeply ingrained in you that you will take more time to spot the feelings and thoughts underlying them.

By working with sadness, or fear or both, you will develop more skillful ways of dealing with your anger. For instance, a thorough analysis can help you identify some unresolved grief. Or you might be struggling with the fear of a certain outcome. With such information, you will be better placed to deal with your anger. It will be easier to determine the best course of action to your unresolved problem. Working with the primary emotion is a way of reducing habitual anger building more inner peace and cultivating thoughtful actions.

Controlled Muscle Relaxation and Deep Breathing

When your emotions are aroused, heart rate and breathing rate are increased. Every emotion has a physical effect and anger normally causes an increase in heart rate, breathing rate, and the release of certain chemicals and hormones in the body. To deal with anger, you need to learn how to control these physical effects. Reversing these physical effects deliberately will ensure that when anger arises, you are in control. Deliberate slow breathing and a systematic relaxation of tensed muscles help a person to control anger.

When angry, you may find that your breaths are shallow and quick. If you allow these shallow breaths to continue, chances are, it will only increase your anger. Instead of allowing the breaths to take control of your body, redirect them into deeper breathing and relax. Practicing deep breaths even when you are not angry will equip you to deal with anger. Set aside some time where you can practice deep breathing exercise. The recommended time for practice is 15 minutes every day. If you practice this exercise for very few times each day, it will be hard to reap the full benefits.

Slow breathing

To start the relaxation efforts, take several deep and slow breaths in a row. Each time, ensure that you exhale for twice as long as the inhalation periods. For instance, if you inhale for 10 seconds, exhale for 20 seconds.

Count slowly to five as you breathe in, then count to eight as you breathe out. As you do this exercise, note the areas where the air is going in the lungs. Breathe deeply and allow air into the full range of your lungs. Your breath should reach your belly first, then your chest and finally to the upper chest and space below the shoulders. In shallow breathing, the air only reaches the upper chest in short spurts. As you take deep breaths, feel your ribs expand as the lungs fill up with air. Pay attention to the way your ribs and lungs relax and go back to their original place as you exhale.

Continue this deep breath process for several minutes. Anytime you feel out of breath or dizzy, ensure that you return to normal. If you have chest problems, It is important to consult a doctor before engaging in this exercise.

Slow, controlled and deliberate breathing will help you to return to normal breathing pace in the event of anger. When the shallow breaths threaten to control you, deep and deliberate breathing will help you to return to the relaxed pattern. Considering that all the things in the body are connected, Chances are, this deep breathing exercise will help to slow down your increasing heart rate, and also to abate the tension in some of your muscles.

Anger often manifests itself in the form of tension in different muscles.

Basically, this tension gathers in the shoulders and neck areas and will stay tensed long after the anger is gone. If you feel the tension gathering in the neck, you can do some exercises to relax. Slowly and gently twist your head to one side then to the other. And make sure you do it GENTLY. Coordinate your breathing with the movement of your head. Roll your head to one side in a gentle motion as you exhale and back to the center as you inhale. Then roll it to the other side as you exhale. Repeat this technique carefully for a number of times – until you feel a little relaxed.

You can release some of the tension in your shoulders by deliberately and gently shrugging your shoulders and relaxing them several times. Rolling the shoulders back and forward can also help you let the tension go. Use these techniques together with the breathing techniques to help let go of anger. As your neck, face and shoulders become more relaxed identify other tensed places in your body and relax. Use an anger management diary to help keep track of the locations in your body where there is tension.

If the muscle relaxation techniques fail to work, try the opposite –

ANGER MANAGEMENT

Tense and tighten that stressed muscles and count slowly to ten. Then, release them. If you feel pain at any one point, make sure that you release the muscles and relax. Move from one group of muscles to the other until you have covered each section of the body. Repeat the process whenever needed.

Once you have practiced this technique for several times, you will be able to cover the entire body within a few minutes. Combining muscle relaxation techniques with eth breathing techniques will help you achieve better relaxation than one technique. In all relaxation efforts, you should give yourself at least 20 – 30 minutes to calm down. During this period, keep your breathing regular and deep. Remind yourself that these efforts are to help you calm down and soon enough, you will feel better.

The relaxation techniques described above can help you calm down and stop focusing on the anger. They will have a positive effect on your body as well as your anger. They also create time for you to rationally think about the situation that was causing you the anger. This time will help you to generate new and fresh solutions to the problems you are facing.

When you feel angry or recognize the onset of anger, try positive self-talk, deep breathing or stopping the angry thoughts line. Breathe deeply and slowly repeat to yourself, calming words such as 'take it easy' or 'relax'. Repeat these terms to yourself while taking deep breaths until the anger reduces.

Seek out help and support from other people. Look for people who can support you in your journey to anger management. Talk about your feelings and try to work on the behavior changes you need to apply.

Whenever someone is making you angry, try to view things from their perspective but putting yourself in their shoes.

If you have a hard time recognizing your anger thoughts and triggers, keep a log, then analyze your feelings and actions.

Although it is better to express anger rather than keep it in, appropriate ways of expression should be applied. Frequent anger outbursts are often counterproductive and often lead to problems in relationships. These outbursts are also harmful to your body – the cardiovascular and nervous system and can make other health problems worse. Learning how to be assertive can help a person to deal with anger, effectively express needs, feelings, and preferences. Being assertive can be very useful in expressing anger rather than acting out ineffectively.

Learning how to see the humor in situations and laughing at yourself can help you to manage anger

Learning how to express your feelings calmly, assert yourself, be direct without being defensive, emotionally charged or hostile.

Consult professionals and read self-help books to understand assertive and effective communication
Practice good listening skills, it will help you to understand people and select the ones you trust. This trust will help you to select the people you should stay close to and the ones you should leave

CHAPTER 5

HOW TO TAKE CONTROL OF YOUR EMOTION AND DEAL WITH ANGER

To take control of your anger, you need to understand the cause and result of anger. People, situations (such as missing a promotion or getting cut off in traffic jam) and circumstances (such as marriage separation or struggling with finances) are the most typical causes of anger. Of the three main causes, people are the main culprits. Family members, partners, children, and other intimate relationships are the main sources of anger. Considering that the people involved in these relationships are very close to a person, it is easy to question why rage gets vented at them. Basically, it is because these relationships are permanent and secure therefore we feel safe to expose our real feelings and emotions.

If you feel that your anger is starting to take a grip on you, there are some steps you can take.

First, your chances of controlling anger are higher if you catch it early enough. When you find yourself in a potential anger triggering situation, emotionally distance yourself from it for a while. Concentrate on the deep breathing exercise. Practice other anger management techniques that might help you handle the situation soberly. Once the anger has subdued, you may continue with the conversation or handling the situation. If the anger keeps getting out of control, give yourself more time - walk away and calm down.

Secondly, look within your heart.

As mentioned earlier, anger tends to stem from deeply rooted things. Sometimes our anger is not caused by the current situation, rather, it stems from other things of the past such as childhood abuse. For men, anger may arise from feeling like a failure. If you are unable to deal with feelings of loss, inadequacy, and insecurity in a productive and positive way, you may release these emotions in the best way you know how.

Basically, this release involves unleashing anger on someone else and blaming them for the current situation. Typically, a loved one is the victim. This expression of feelings may come off as controlling. To deal with such feelings, tell yourself that dominating others doesn't amount to power rather, acknowledging difficult emotions and dealing with them in a respectful way. Remember that regardless of how a person is winding you up, the choice of how you react is absolutely yours.

Thirdly, switch your focus

When you concentrate on the situation that is angering you, it becomes harder to stay in control. Instead of focusing on the situation, pay attention to the physical sensations occurring in your body. The most common responses to feelings of anger include headaches, rapid breathing, clenched jaws or fists, and tensed muscles. According to psychotherapists, concentrating on physical sensations rather than the emotional pressure will help you to control your anger. Once you have taken note of these physical sensations, focus on easing them. Go for a walk or do some physical exercise which will help you get rid of the pent-up energy. Relax the tensed muscles by gently massaging the affected areas such as the neck or shoulders. Visualization can also help you switch your focus – imagine yourself in a calm and happy place.

Fourthly, lighten the mood.

When you use humor appropriately, it will help to diffuse anger. A lighter mood will help you deal with issues more constructively. For instance, if your boss is yelling at you because of a particular thing, imagine him/her as a funny cartoon character dancing. Draw a picture of him/her if it helps. If this practice can help you diffuse anger and think more constructively, then use it often. However, ensure that you do not use the humor in a sadistic way – Mood lightening should not be used to bring other people down. The reason for using humor as an anger management technique is to stop taking yourself and others too seriously.

Anger is a most present pressing and somehow painful force in our lives. Even though we as men are not allowed to display our emotions every now and then, they drive us day to day. Emotions make us take new chances. We are excited because of new and possible prospects. We make sacrifices for love and cry when we are hurt. Without a doubt, our thoughts, emotions, intentions, and actions are interconnected and with the authority of rational minds, we are able to make valid choices. However, when we act on negative emotions too quickly, we often make decisions which we later regret.

Our emotions and feelings can switch between dangerous extremities. Stagger too far on one side and you are on the verge of rage. Steer too far in the other direction and you will border the state of euphoria. As with many other things in life, emotions are best dealt with logically and moderately. Everything in excess is poisonous. Honestly speaking, it can be hard to control feelings of joy. After receiving great news, it can be hard to not feel too joyous and jump of joy. It is also okay to fall in love. These are the good things in life and we can celebrate them. What we should really aim to control are the negative emotions. These must be handled with extra care.

Negative emotions like anger and rage tend to spin out of control very fast especially immediately after they have been activated. Gradually, these emotions can grow like undesirable weeds and gradually condition the mind function on them. Anger and other negative feelings can dominate daily life and become detrimental. The worst part is that these feelings feed on themselves. One angry thought normally leads to another. Ever realized that a hostile person seems to be in an angry trigger happy state at all times? Well, they were not born like that. This anger is just a habit they took up and allowed to grow. When negative emotions stir in us for too long, they become inbred, rising all too often.

So, how can we master anger when it arises in the harshest of circumstances? How can we avoid operating on the negative types of feelings? Below are some steps you may follow to control anger and reestablish rationality in a challenging situation.

a. Do not react right away.

In a challenging moment (for instance when a situation is triggering anger) our first thought is to act immediately. In fact, emotions are so fast that they hinder us from having rational thoughts before acting. It is guaranteed that a moment of anger can make you say or do things you will later regret. To avoid reacting an a regrettable way, it is important to not react immediately. Before countering the trigger, with an argument based only on emotions and irrational thoughts, take a deep breath, relax and stabilize the impulse. Continue to take deep breaths for a while, and use the muscle relaxation techniques to release some of the tension clouding your judgment. Feel your heart rate as it goes back to normal. As you become calmer, remind yourself that the situation is only temporally, think clearly, then speak up.

b. Ask for divine intervention.

Regardless of the creed we believe in, faith is our saving grace. It helps us in the darkest moments. As such, developing a healthy and strong relationship with a divine world of your choice can help you overcome obstacles more easily. This is because; having a divine connection will help you to stay in control. Believing in a bigger power will help you to seek for guidance. Divine intervention will show you what to do in moments of anger. When burdened with a hard situation, close your eyes and envision a positive solution given to you through divine intervention. Ask the divine power to show you how to go about your problem.

c. Find a healthy outlet

Once you have gotten control of your anger, - you no longer act out thoughtlessly, you will need to identify a healthy way of letting it go. Emotions and more so anger should never be suppressed. Bottling anger up only builds on the pressure in our lives and might lead us into depression. So, to deal with this anger, share what happened with someone you trust. Ensure that the person you are telling will not rub salt to the injury. Having an opinion from another person can help you to look at things more clearly. Your awareness becomes more broadened.

You may also keep a journal where you express your feelings. Some people find it helpful to engage in aggressive exercises, for instance, martial arts and kickboxing. Although it is not always advisable to use aggression to let go of anger, sometimes this form of expression may help. However, one has t do it with moderation. Other people find it more helpful to engage in chanting and meditation to return to a state of tranquility. Do whatever exercise that takes your mind off the anger and any other pent up sentiments. Everything you do needs moderation.

d. See the bigger picture

Everything that happens in our lives serves a higher purpose. It does not matter whether the situation is good or bad, there is a reason. Wisdom is the ability to see beyond the current situation. It is the ability to get a greater meaning in any given situation. Sometimes you may just imagine a positive result. For instance, you may imagine that the driver who cut you off o the freeway just protected you from an accident that was brewing ahead. You may not really understand what is happening at the beginning of the situation but as time goes by, everything will fit perfectly in the bigger picture. It can be hard to see a bigger picture in the midst of intense emotions but trust that there is an ultimate purpose which will be revealed in time.

e. Replace your thoughts

Our thoughts determine our actions. Negative emotions will lead us to more negative thoughts and actions. This creates a cycle of downright negative thoughts patterns. Whenever a negative thought seems to consume your brain, push it out and select another positive thing to think about. Imagine the best-fitted solution to your problem playing out perfectly in your head. Think about a thing or person that makes you happy and inspired and let it overrun the negative thought.

f. Forgive your triggers.

There are people or events that trigger your emotions. A trigger of your anger may be a parent, best friend, work colleague, spouse, yourself, or a group of people. You may feel a strong wave of anger when a person does 'that thing' you hate so much. Forgive him or her. You may feel angry when you remember something that you did, probably costing you an opportunity – forgive yourself. This forgiveness should come with a detachment. Detach yourself from the fury, jealousy or resentment receding within you.

Negative emotions cohabit. You will find that anger goes hand in hand with resentment and anxiety. Letting go of one negative emotion will help you to release the others. Allow people to be themselves without getting emotional. If someone behaves like a pain, let them be, without allowing their behavior to disturb your peace. You do not have to have escalated negative emotions every time. As you forgive, it becomes easier to disassociate from harsh feelings.

A constant reminder of our nature, emotions surges through our bodies every second of the day. Sadly, we often take negative actions when experiencing anger. It is time we restrain wrong feelings from filtering through our minds. To avoid the pain of acting out during an emotional uproar, take some simple steps to tame your heightened anger and calm your uneasy mind. Once you look at the moment after it has passed, you will be more grateful that you can master your emotions.

CHAPTER 6

DON'T HOLD GRUDGES

Being hurt by someone can cause sadness, confusion, and anger. These feelings are more intense if the person who hurt us is a loved one. Relationships can suffer when a person has trouble forgiving the other, especially in close relationships. Dwelling on the thing that causes you to hurt will only lead to anger. Holding a grudge and being unable to solve the problem causes anger and many angry people have trouble forging those who wronged them. They use the grudge to justify their anger feelings and unfair behavior. Instead of letting go, they continue to re-experience the pain, frustration, and resentment.

Human beings are a very unique and self-preserving species whereby, once a person has been wronged, he/she wants the offender to acknowledge the deed. If the offender fails to own the mistake, we tend to get angry and want the world to know. In fact, we want the party to pay for their wrong actions. This continuous dwelling on the wrong deeds done against us fuels anger. So, is wanting to make other people accountable for their actions a bad thing? Partially, yes. To put it simply, the need to make a person pay for his/her mistakes leads to a grudge. And the more you want revenge, the more the anger arises.

The reason for holding a grudge may seem worth and valid to you. Truthfully, you were extremely upset and the offensive person deserves to feel some wrath. How could that person make you feel so bad? It is in our nature to want revenge. But is the wrongdoer or his/her actions really worth destroying your own health? Mahatma Gandhi once said that forgiveness is a character for the strong. Everyone needs a lot of courage to move on from a hurtful experience inflicted on you by another person. But if you let go of all that grudge and anger, you will be bettering your life and health. Forgiveness will make your life happier in many ways. Some of the reasons why it is better to let go of grudges include:

1. Holding onto grudges could harm your heart

According to research conducted and published by the American Heart Association, high levels of anger may increase your risk of getting coronary heart disease, more so in older men. Even after adjusting for other risky behaviors such as cigarette smoking, anger increases the risk of heart diseases. Bottling up anger due to grudges will take a serious till on the physical health. Another report conducted by Men's Health in 2013 suggests that repressing feelings of anger can lead to high blood pressure.

2. Showing rage will make an impression on children

Young children normally mold their behavior according to their environment, and this is more evident when it comes to anger and hostility. Now, unless you want to raise angry children, it is better for you to keep off anger. According to research published in the Cognitive Development Journal, babies can not only sense danger in their environment, but they also learn to adjust to it very fast. What makes the matter more interesting is that children have a long memory yet their brains cannot rationalize emotions. The study found that toddlers had the ability to classify people prone to anger according to previous anger outbursts.

3. Even a short episode of anger can cause negative health implications.

Holding onto anger can easily threaten your wellbeing but we should also note that short term anger could also anger you. According to a research conducted by Harvard School of Public Health, a subject is five times more likely to have a heart attack and three times the risk of a stroke in the two hours following an outburst of anger.

4. It messes with your mental health.

Situations leading to an upset have a way of putting the real state of our minds at stake. This stalling leads us into a spiral of thoughts that affect our mental health. Anger has a strange way of increasing stress and anxiety. According to psychologists, holding onto these negative emotions can turn into something more dangerous.

In the times of our ancestors, anger helped people to stand their ground and fight. However, in today's technologically complex world, anger more of a hindrance than a help. The level of anger affects the clarity of thought. The angrier you are, the less likely you are to think. Consequently, your negotiation skills lower, your ability to take a different perspective is affected thus you have a harder time handling a provocation.

5. Anger has been linked to type 2 diabetes

According to information published by the National Institute of Health, anger potentially leads to diabetes through unhealthy practices. While there is no direct connection between temperament and immediate diabetes risk, there are some studies and findings worth noting. In the study conducted by the National Institute of heath, the people with the highest levels of anger also had 34 percent increased of getting diabetes 2 unlike those with lower anger levels. Basically, people with chronic anger are more likely to take higher levels of calories and to smoke and these two factors could lead to the development of type 2 diabetes.

6. Holding onto grudges can cause stress

It is already very difficult to actually live through a hard time/ trying situation but letting go of the difficult things maybe even leading to further damage. Anger and bitterness can lead to increases heart rate and higher levels of stress. The cure - forgiveness. Researches have revealed that pardoning others can create lower physiological stress responses. It is also important to forgive yourself.

- Letting go of a grudge will help you to rise

Turns out, holding onto grudges and anger will continuously weigh you down emotionally, mentally as well as physically. In an experiment conducted and published in the journal of social psychosocial and personality science, people who choose to forgive tend to jump higher than those who held grudges. The burden of anger is normally more than just a physical thing.

- It will help you to sleep better

Everyone wants to get more restful sleep rather than tossing and turning around in bed for seemingly endless hours. According to a study conducted in 205 on better sleep, subjects were found to have better sleep and quality rest when they let go of the resentment.

- Forgiveness will help you strengthen your social bonds

Letting go of anger and resentment will also improve your relationships. As we all know, having healthy relationships is very important for a good life. Having this in mind, part of forgiveness is asking for it and also letting go. Asking for forgiveness normally requires a degree of modesty. That sense of humility will without a doubt make your relationships stronger. Researches also indicate that forgiveness will help the two parties to refocus on their goals and create a deeper bond of love.

The way to freedom from anger or grudges is not only through the forgiveness of the other person but also through loving your own self. We need to bring our own caring and loving self to the situation that crystalized into a grudge and anger. The pain caused by others will only be melted by our own decision to stay positive. That is the only way we can move forward. Sometimes it can be hard to move from our current state of holding grudges, therefore, we need to ask for help from our loved ones. The idea of letting go off the grudge is to deal with the pain without re-traumatizing self. We need to give ourselves the compassion we are looking for through holding grudges. Bring your own self-love to the center of the storm. Our hearts hold pain, but they also hold the cure to the pain.

To let go of the grudge, you need to move your focus from the wrongdoer, away from the sad story and suffering and into the fact that we lived through it. When you shift your attention from the pain in your heart to the lesson learned and the strength acquired from living through the storm, it becomes easier to look at the wrongdoing as a story. It stops being too personal – you learn how to let go.

In changing our attention span from the wrongdoing, we find that soothing compassion that the grudge needed to heal. Additionally, we should take responsibility for caring and healing our own sufferings, and for understanding that our happiness matters more than our sufferings.

Happiness can never be achieved through holding grudges and losing tempers no matter how fiercely we believe in revenge. Forgiveness is the only way to right the wrong we feel so strongly. Once we let go of the need to hold grudges, it becomes easy to drop away anger even without realizing it. What becomes clearer is, we are complete in our own hearts.

How to let go

One interesting thing that makes us want to hold grudges is that it feels like a sweater or blanket – covering our weaknesses and keeping us warm. And getting rid of it leaves us feeling naked. We can all agree that forgiveness sometimes feels like a weakness. The challenge is, that grudge is more of a worn-out piece of cloth which only irritates us. In fact, a grudge becomes so strong that it develops a life of its own. However, the lightness and relief accompanying forgiveness are amazing.

Unforgiven offenders

It could be the uncaring Parent, the unfaithful partner, the ex-best friend who hurt you, the criminal who abused you, the workplace bully or any other person. You have every reason to hold grudges against the person but now what?

After betrayals like infidelity, or physical abuse by a bully, the urge to protect oneself from further pain or hurt becomes basic. That kind of hurt makes us recognize that we are vulnerable, hurt and most probably out of power. That vulnerability is what we try to avoid from that moment onwards. It is okay to avoid that position where we got hurt.

Consequently, we hang onto that hurt and keep it as a bargaining chip. For instance, you may tell your spouse "Do not even try to complain about me yet you can remember ---"

Continuing to keep your loved ones at a distance just because of suspicions and mistrust will prevent you from achieving a deeper and more satisfying relationship. Holding a grudge will make you not to forgive even when the wrongdoer apologizes and changes his/her behaviors actively.

Sometimes, we never get to receive the apology we expected from the wrongdoer. In fact, the person who wronged us might never show even a drop of remorse for what they did. This forms scar tissue in us. We eventually want to hold out the fact that someone offended us so that the world can see and sympathize with our aches. We seek understanding and caring from others in an effort to heal from what we did not get an apology for. Instead of becoming stronger, we become sentimental- more about "I was wronged therefore I deserve to be pitied."

Grudges and anger have a corrosive effect on your physical and emotional health. Being angry all the time keeps you stuck in the fight or flight mode. Lack of forgiveness keeps you in the same anger position for a long time. The hormones released in the body during this state can cause increased heart rate and blood pressure.

ANGER MANAGEMENT

And all the other untrusting and negative mentality will spill into and affect other relationships.

The basic steps for letting a grudge go

Grudges take time to root and grow therefore letting go is also a process. Some of the steps one may follow to let go of grudges include;

- Acknowledge the hurt- It is true that you were wronged. In fact, you have every right to feel hurt. Describing the events that lead to your hurt and how you actually felt can help you get a better understanding of your situation. You may write it in a journal or a letter to yourself. Tell the truth in that writing will help you to heal. You may also imagine the wrongdoer seated in a chair and tell them exactly how you feel. Also, give yourself credit for all the steps you took to get where you have gotten.

- Decide to forgive – Forgiving a person who has hurt you is a reward to yourself. Notre that forgiving the offender does not mean that you have forgotten the deed. In fact, it does not mean that you should entertain further offenses from people. Forgive the wrongdoers and take the necessary steps to protect yourself. Deciding to forgive does not mean that the offender will start acting differently. It does not mean that the person who wronged you will actually admit to the wrong did. It is not your business to make the person sorry. Forgiveness means letting the matter go.

It might even need you to forgive yourself first before getting a way of forgiving others.

- Realize that forgiving does not mean condoning more wrong deeds

Accepting does not mean agreeing. Sometimes you may accept the opinion of another person even if you do not agree with him/her. In cases of grudges, we are afraid of letting go because of the assumption that the offender will feel that he/she has won. Note that acceptance only means that you have forgiven the person. After all, you cannot go back and change the past.

- Ask yourself: Why?

Basically, people feel that anger and grudges are a burden when they realize that their own development is being stalled. It becomes boring to keep talking about an old event that happened to you yet the wrongdoer does not even care. It feels bad to keep rewinding the same scenes in your head and turning the hurt in your heart. The grievance begins to feel old and even the people around you no longer pay attention to your complaining. It does not matter anymore. Yet strangely enough, letting go feels like a threat. You have already taken the default stand of a victim- "This happened to me and I'm still hurting." You may also fear that letting go will make you feel empty. Why then is it so important to let go of the anger and grudge? To create room for good things and have healthier and more positive feelings in your life.
- Consider a positive trade-off

ANGER MANAGEMENT

In order to let go easily, take stock of the benefits that will accrue to you after forgiveness. Know that letting go of the anger will give you peace and extra personal energy. All the time you spent turning over the pain in your heart will be used for positive gains. Forgiving will give you a sense of freedom and an ability to trust and rebuild a more genuine relationship.

- Do not allow anger to define you

Anger can block your progress. You can actually be defined by the grudges you hold. These feelings will keep you stuck in the same location. Even if you feel that the offender must be punished. It is important to forgive him/her for the wrong deed for your own freedom. For instance, the people in the South Carolina shoot out chose to forgive the shooter even if they still wanted him to face the law. Do not let the offenses define your life, there are so many good things waiting for you ahead.

- Pay attention to the feedback you are getting

Firstly, if the people around you suggest that you are getting stuck, it is time to start a new narrative. Even the most patient and compassionate listeners get weary of complaints. When you hold onto a grudge, there are high chances that you will keep repeating your grievance story. Once you hear your friends or relatives complain about your behavior or narratives, you need to find a new line.
- Change the conversation

If you are the confidant of a person who is holding a grudge, it is upon you to help him move on. For instance, instead of concentrating only on the situation leading to the grudge and the details of the offense, deepen your curiosity and assess why the person needs to stay stuck on the past yet we are in the present moment. If you have listened to the complainer enough, it is okay to tell him/her with compassion and kindness that you cannot keep hearing the same sad story and that he/she needs to change.

- Practice letting go

Empathy enables one to forgive. Recognize the perspective of the other person. Understand that everyone has some unresolved pain or issue. Note that when a person acts in his/her self-interest, there are high chances of conflicting with your interests. Such knowledge can help you deal with anger and grudges. You know that it is not every action hurting you that is deliberately designed to make you feel bad. Some of the practices you can use to let go include visualization, daily affirmation meditation, journal writing and monitoring your attitude and thoughts will help. Try picturing a rope that is connecting you to the wrongdoer then let it go. Imagine yourself carrying a big unnecessary stone in your heart then drop it in a dark hole.

- Let go of the victimhood state

You can spend years ranting and raving about an event that took place a long time ago but the truth is, it will not make your life better. If you keep complaining about your childhood, then you will not be able to move on to better things in adulthood. At least you will not achieve your full potential. You will find that everything that happens to you leads back to one issue … the person that hurt you. Feeling like you are always hurt and pissed off will not serve any positive purpose. If anything, you will always be vulnerable. Everything happening in your life will feel personal and forgiveness will be very hard. It is therefore very important to let go of the role of the victim and be in charge of your own life.

- Embrace yourself

Having the power to let go of grudge results in transformation and elevation. Once you drop the victimhood role, you discover a different person in you. Beneath that anger is a person who is capable of love, someone who is textured and layered with positive energy. Love and appreciate the person you have become after letting the grudges go.

- Build on grace

There is an advanced form of forgiveness referred to as grace. It is the ability to have prepackaged forgiveness. In simple terms, grace is having the ability to pull out forgiveness from a shelf even when it is least deserved. Such strength will help you to keep close relations with people even when they wrong you. In fact, you will be able to influence other people with your positive energy. Grace will help you to bypass grudges all together.

CHAPTER 7

IDENTIFYING WHAT CAUSES YOUR ANGER

When dealing with anger, it is important to understand the things that trigger this emotion. At the most basic level, anger can be used to help protect family members, loved ones and territories from harm. It can also be used to respond to perceived and real threats and protect against losses.

Other causes of anger can be very diverse depending on the people involved and while some of them are rational and justifiable, others are completely irrational. Simply put, irrational anger might indicate that you have a problem with anger management and even accepting that you need help.

Some of the questions you can answer to help you recognize your anger include;
How do I recognize that I am angry?
What are my reactions when I am upset?
Which places, people or events make me angry?
How does my anger affect other people and my relationships?

ANGER MANAGEMENT

Some of the common triggers of anger include;

1. Loss, grief, sadness, death of a loved one,
2. Tiredness, - people with short tempers are more likely to lose their temper when tired or irritable
3. Rudeness, poor services, and interpersonal skills
4. Hunger
5. Injustice
6. Sexual frustration
7. A feeling of disappointment or failure
8. Some forms of stress, loss of control, unrealistic deadlines
9. becoming angry because of drug abuse and also withdraw symptoms
10. being physically or mentally unwell especially when suffering from a serious chronic illness.
11. Crimes committed against you or your loved ones.

Considering that there are many reasons why one can get angry or have anger management issues, it is important to have an anger plan.

An anger plan involves tools that can help you keep track of the causes and rating of your anger. This plan helps a person to identify and diffuse anger in a timely manner before it gets out of control. In order to take control of your anger, you will want to list out things you can participate in to calm down.

For instance, part of an anger plan may involve taking time out once you start feeling upset, to remove yourself from the anger-provoking situation. Another tool that you may use to shift from anger is to change the conversation to a more neutral topic. An anger plan ensures that you have an understanding of your situation and a way of escaping.

There are a lot of things which one can do to deal with an anger situation once he is willing to take control. The best of these techniques will help a person to deal with the anger and stay calm without damaging his/ her pride. Because each person has unique strengths and weaknesses, the anger plan will differ for different individuals.

Anger Diary

Point to note: Anger rating will help you to understand the intensity of anger at different times. However, they do not help you to predict the situations that will cause you anger in the first place. That is why an anger diary is important.

As the saying goes, prevention is better than cure. In order to prevent a certain thing from occurring, you need to understand what causes it in the first place. Being able to predict the specific situations that might bring about upsets can help you to keep your temper under control. When you identify these situations, you have a choice to avoid them completely, or, gather the best tools for handling the unavoidable ones. Knowing that a particular situation will trigger anger helps you to prepare with ways of minimizing risk.

ANGER MANAGEMENT

An anger diary is very useful when you want to keep track of your anger experiences. You will need to make daily entries of situations that provoked your ANGER. Documenting these situations will help you to make comparisons and keep track of your progress. In order to have a useful diary, there is some information you need to record for each situation.

First, what exactly happened that lead you to feel stressed and pained? What exactly made you angry?
Secondly, what part of the situation was provocative? Which parts were not provocative?
Thirdly, what were you thinking at that point? What was taking place in your brain?
How angry did you feel? Rate your rage between 1 and 100. What was the effect of your actions and reactions at this point?
Was there another thing making you nervous, tensed or pressured at this point? If so, what was it?
Was the reaction really warranted at this point?
What were your physical reactions? Did your heart rate increase? Did your muscles become tense? Were your palms sweating?
Did you want to fight or flight?
Did you throw things around, become verbally abusive? Slam the doors?
Did you scream or turn the anger on another person?
How did you feel during and after the anger episode?
Did you feel different later after losing your temper?
What were the consequences of this incident?
Are the consequences justifiable?

ANGER MANAGEMENT

After keeping track of this information for a period of time, say, a week or two, review it and look for the reoccurring themes. What triggers consistently made you mad? All triggers fall into one of these several categories

- Other people doing or failing to do what is expected of them
- People taking advantage of you
- Situations and people that are getting in your way,
- Being disappointed and angry with yourself
- A combination of these categories.

Also, look for those reoccurring thoughts that trigger your anger again and again. You can identify these thoughts particularly because they involve one or two of these lines;

- The belief that a person was trying to provoke you
- A person intentionally wronged you.
- The perception that you have been harmed or victimized.
- The belief that the other person was on the wrong yet he/she failed to admit.
- The belief that a person should have behaved differently in order to achieve success in a particular thing.

Use the anger diary to track instances where you felt angered or harmed, why you felt harmed, if and why you think the act was deliberate and why it was wrong. Identifying your thought patterns will help you to see the commonalities between themes and your anger. Some examples of thoughts triggering your anger include;

People are rude, inconsistent and untrustworthy,
People do not pay enough attention to the needs of others and they hardly care about you.
People expect or demand too much from you
People are mean and cruel
People disrespect, shame and criticize you
People use you or take advantage of your good spirit
People are mean or cruel
People refuse to do their share or take responsibility
People try to manipulate or control you
People are stupid or incompetent
People make you wait

Below are some situations where these thoughts might occur;

1. When receiving and expressing negative thoughts.
2. When expressing a different opinion
3. When saying no
4. When protesting
5. When proposing an idea
6. When asking for cooperation
7. When responding to criticism
8. When speaking about something that angers you
9. When dealing with an uncooperative person

Underlying all these trigger thoughts is the mentality that other people are behaving in the wrong manner and you have every right to be angry and act out. All trigger thoughts seem to pass the blame to other people and none to you. In most cases, people will identify a line of thought or pattern that fuels their anger. Look for the instances where your anger rose and look for similarities and similar triggering thoughts making you lose your temper.

The purpose of your diary is to facilitate your process of identifying the recurring behavioral elements and patterns that really push your anger off the table. The more accurately you can trace and observe your behaviors and feelings, the higher the chances of control. The more detailed your diary is, the better your chances of finding your triggers accurately and finding your control. Understanding the way your anger operates will help you to come up with a planned strategy for coping with the different emotions in a more productive way.

Once you have spotted some of the things triggering your anger, and the different themes, you will be better positioned to work constructively towards controlling your anger. Your response to these triggers is the main area you needed to monitor. Anger triggering thoughts arise automatically and in most cases, instantaneously. Anger management requires you to become conscious of your thoughts and actions regardless of the situation. You need to deliberately work towards identifying the moment when anger starts to rise and take control before things get out of hand.

For instance, imagine someone cuts you off while you are driving on a freeway yet you want to beat the clock and arrive at a meeting in time. Take note of the physical reactions letting you know just how upset you are at that moment. Once you notice these feelings, the next step is to apply an anger control plan. First, take a deep breath.

Secondly, try to think about the situation in a rational way. See, your first reaction normally involves the impulse to attack. Kin anger management, you should consciously redirect your thoughts and instead of thinking that the driver deliberately cut you off to make you late, look at it as a mistake. Maybe the driver did not see you in the first place. If you choose to think that the issue at hand was a mistake rather than an intentional offense, it becomes easier to forgive and tolerate.

When you feel justified to feel angry, you give yourself permission to be upset, even though the reason for it is not warranted. The sooner you stop justifying your anger the faster it will recede. While you might have every reason to be angry or to hold a grudge, there is no justification for acting inappropriately due to loss of a temper. Remember that being angry is not good for your health either. In fact, it destroys all your important relationships.

CHAPTER 8

BE RESPONSIBLE FOR YOUR ANGER

We tend to blame others for our behavior especially when angry. That is why we found that most triggers of anger result from our opinion of others. For instance, one can claim that he is angry because someone insulted him, or another one is rude and self-centered. "If he did not say that, I would not have beaten her". "If my father had been there for me, I would be a better person." "If she can respect me, I would never be abusive e to her."

These are some of the examples you might have heard during your lifetime as angry people make excuses for their state and behavior. We all try to justify our anger by pointing at the weaknesses and errors of other people. Basically, we do anything to avoid taking the blame for the way we express our anger.

Imagine a case where a husband d hits his wife after threatening to get a divorce. The husband can claim that he was under the influence of alcohol or that his wife is too nagging thus forcing him to act drastically. This aggressive behavior is actually a way of covering the hurt powerlessness and fear he is feeling. Instead of acknowledging that the marriage is not working (And the part he played in the failure) and then working towards a solution, the man chooses to live in denial thus passing the blame to wife and alcohol.

Another good example would be that of a driver cutting another person off on a freeway. An angry person can take this act personally and claim that the driver did that intentionally. Basically, that assumption will trigger other negative feelings that were already there before the incidence. If you had a good morning in the house before leaving for work, chances are, you will not get angry because someone has cut you off on the road. However, if you had an argument with someone in the morning before leaving the house, you will harbor those angry feelings and when someone makes you angry or cuts you off on the freeway, you will take it personally. In fact, you will act out in an unexpected way.

In other cases, people choose to blame their childhood for the way they turned out. It is very easy for a person to blame a parent or guardian for who they turned out to be. What such persons fail to realize is that they have grown up and are responsible for their own behavior. There comes a time when you can no longer point at the modeling you observed while growing up. There comes a time when you know the difference between what is good and bad.

In each of the mentioned cases, the angry person denies responsibility for his behavior. He portrays himself as a helpless powerless and weak person who is incapable of change. Each person has a different form of anger and a way of passing the blame. However, every one of them fails to recognize the role he played towards the current situation. This tendency to blame other people only strengthens the self-perception of powerlessness and consequently, waters a higher likelihood of blaming others.

Suggesting that an event contributed to your anger is okay. However, it is a different issue to pass all the blame to other people and act as if we are entirely helpless. It is not okay to make other people responsible for the intensity of our feelings and our behaviors.

Why do we tend to blame other people?

Most of our habits in adulthood can be traced to early childhood development. The tendency to blame other people for our mistakes normally develops from a tender age. Some of us learn how to pass the blame from observing our parents. Others learn how to blame others as a defense mechanism. If a person was shamed or punished for admitting responsibility for something that turned out wrong, he will look for ways to escape the blame. Consequently, he learns how to blame other people. Perhaps we never develop a capacity to deal with our own feelings when something turns out as unexpected. Maybe we have never learned ways to accept our failures even when others criticize us.

Blaming other people for our anger and reactions be it individuals or societies can be traced back to the early days. History has it that human beings want to see themselves as better than others. That is why nations got into wars, and people went to fight each other. It is a battle for the conquest and when one fails, he will look for a scapegoat – something/someone to accuse. We want to see ourselves as flawless and better than we truly are. Passing the blame helps us to justify the actions we could consider as a weakness. For instance, losing a war makes a country appear weak but claiming that the winning country used corrupt ways to win helps the looser to avoid looking at its flaws.

Destructive anger, in general, is a defense mechanism. Blaming others for our ways of handling anger is also a strategy we use to avoid experiencing and recognizing difficult and challenging feelings such as guilt, shame, disappointment, hurt, sadness, inadequacy, and powerlessness. Passing the blame to other people is a way of self-defense – a strategy of deception used with the intention of preserving our self-esteem. It involves an attempt to deny the real situation and feelings which we judge as too uncomfortable. Blaming other people helps us to get away from shame. Blame, especially that arising from anger also reflects the need to disown our responsibility for our behaviors.

Blaming other people for our anger can also be considered 'blame avoidance' and like any other defense mechanism, it can be classified under 'emotional avoidance' whereby we avoid feeling the full intense and powerful emotions.

Additionally, blaming others for the ways we express anger enhances our sense of righteousness and perfection. Since we do not have to acknowledge our actions and their consequences when blaming others, we see ourselves as flawless and justified.

For people with chronic anger, blame is often used not only to express anger but also in other sectors of life. The blame game can help a chronically angry person to save face when they feel weak or flawed.

Consequences of blaming other people for how we handle anger

1. When we blame others for the way we deal with anger, we fail to experience genuine and true empowerment. Blaming others only keeps a person away from taking responsibility for his actions. Basically passing the blame only diminishes your power of being self-sufficient and builds on your sense of victimhood. In other words, you become weaker and unable to develop a stronger feeling of self-reliance. You are unable to deal with other feelings like guilt, fear, and anxiety.

When you continuously perceive yourself as a victim, you unknowingly foster stronger feelings of helplessness, powerlessness, and pessimism – all these negative feelings will increase the proneness for anger arousal. Blaming others normally reduces autonomy and our free will to make choices. Consequently, we experience reduced freedom, and higher chances of losing our tempers over and over again.

2. Blaming others may also be viewed as a way of thriving on as well as contributing towards dependency. Genuinely speaking, taking responsibility for our actions is not always an easy task. In fact, admitting that we are flawed can easily arouse the feeling of anxiety. We might worry about what other people will think of us after they know about the other side. Taking responsibility can heighten our sense of loneliness as well as confusion. We become unsure of the decisions and choices we make in life. This kind of feelings fuel our need to blame others for our anger. We depend on blame games to explain our position to ourselves and others.

3. Failing to take responsibility distracts us form self-reflection. Basically, the blame game will keep you away from the challenging task of self-stock take. You will not see the need to reflect on your actions since there is someone else taking the blame. After all, another person made you act the way you did in the first place. Self-reflection is a difficult task because it reveals things about yourself which you might not want to really deal with. However, it is an important and crucial part of our lives and will enable us to take responsibility. Self-reflection expands our sense of choice and responsibility while blaming others constricts it. Through self-reflection, we are in a better place to define our desires and realize how to satisfy them. We develop constructive connections with ourselves through self-reflection. And this informs the choices we make about our lives.

4. Blaming other people contributes to feelings of powerlessness and helplessness. Holding someone else responsible for our actions only diminishes the openness of reflection and drains away power. These feelings of helplessness and powerlessness do not only lead to anger but also to depression. In recent researches, anger has been identified as an indicator of depression, more so in men. As such, while passing the blame might help one to avoid feelings such as guilt or anxiety, it only increases the chances of depression through increased levels of helplessness and hopelessness.

5. Blaming other people may reflect global thinking. This is more applicable in cases where a person shows his anger towards a certain group of people. some angry people will accuse whole ethnic groups, religions, races, and sexualities for the major difficulties in life. Some people will even blame strangers for their misfortunes. Such scapegoating only shows a global perspective that increases our sense of powerlessness and reactivity. It fosters a deep renunciation of responsibility that will further support a justification for aggression. Additionally, this scapegoating leads to the demonization of others supporting dehumanization.

6. Blaming others for our character robs us the opportunity to have stronger resilience t better deal with life changes and challenges. Every time we accuse someone else for our anger management

failures, we miss the opportunity to examine the ways through which we get in our own way. In the process, we fail to actually move towards our goals. The lack of resilience leaves us unable to satisfy our key desires. Every time we blame others for our anger, we miss the opportunity to grow personally.

7. Blaming leads to more blaming. Researches on brain mechanisms have found that the more we have certain behaviors and thoughts, the more they become part of the neuronal pathways in our brains. Therefore, the more we blame others for our behaviors, the more we will continue to blame them. And the more we will have a reason to respond aggressively. Finally, anger and aggression will be a go-to reaction without hesitation.

What is the antidote to blame?

We all know that life is challenging. All of us have experienced some percentage of suffering. Everyone has weaknesses and flaws and we tend to make mistakes. All of these aspects make us human. What then can we use as an antidote to blame? We can cultivate self-compassion. This involves learning to fully acknowledge our human nature. Self-compassion helps us to accept and acknowledge our thoughts and feelings with positive curiosity rather than judgment. It also supports our ability to respond and acknowledge our pain rather than ignore, deny, minimize or suppress it. Compassion can help us to accept all parts of ourselves instead of disowning those things we find not befitting.

Additionally, building on compassion entails evoking wisdom and mindfulness to locate what is in our best interests. This compassion also helps us to engage in self-reflection which is very essential for us to deeply connect with our inner selves. Deep connections with ourselves help us to identify who we are and who we aim to become. Compassion involves turning inward and asking yourself what you can do to improve your situation. Such self-assessment is crucial especially during suffering' Compassion further supports our ability to engage in solitude – which is a state allowing for self-reflection and increased self-awareness.

Some of the steps you can take to reduce the tendency of blaming others include;

a) Recognize the blame when it occurs,
b) Reflect on the reason you are passing the blame. What feelings are you avoiding through blaming another person?
c) Cultivate self-compassion and increase self-awareness. You are only human and bound to make mistakes, have weaknesses, and flaws.
d) Recognize how global thinking contributes to your blame habits
e) Assess your contributions to your anger and behavior.
f) Identify what you can do to deal with your anger in a more constructive way and address your suffering.
g) Experiment with the feelings that scare you such as vulnerability and fear.

h) Practice assertive communication. Talk about how you were impacted by the situation rather than how someone made you feel.
i) Be aware of any negative criticism or self-talk you experience while dealing with the blame issues.

Your tendency to blame others may have provided you some form of protection from uncomfortable feelings such as fear and anxiety. Because this blaming becomes a habit, a way of thinking, a deeply ingrained practice, it takes some time to let go. Each habit that is learned can be changed. However, you will need a lot of motivation and discipline to let go of these protective defenses. Since these blame tendencies are deeply established within the self, you may need professional help you deal with them.

Reducing blaming habits can be very invigorating. This process will help a person to take back his mental energy thus understand the landscape of his inner self. Further, we are able to develop resilience in dealing with the most difficult challenges in life.

Taking responsibility

Epictetus said that we cannot choose our circumstances but we can always choose how we react to them. Though our feelings are subject to the influence of external events, these events have no value by themselves. We are the people who attach value to circumstances. Our attitudes are influenced by how we perceive the world, and consequently, our behaviors for instance, if we assume that every person has the intention of hurting or using us, chances are we will always take the defense. Our attitude towards everyone will be selfish.

In simpler terms, we are fundamentally accountable for the beliefs and attitudes that represent our world view; that is, what is worthwhile, good, fearful, significant, pleasant, horrible et cetera. Then this means that we are responsible for our actions. Taking responsibility for our actions is a crucial step for personal growth and a significant element in managing difficult situations in life. Being responsible helps us to control our feelings, more so anger.

What is the role of accountability in anger management? Anger is considered to be one of the most difficult emotions to deal with especially when it gets out of control. Angry behavior is normally an indicator of lack of control. It shows that the person has unresolved issues. On the other hand personal responsibility is an indicator of proactivity towards regaining control of our lives. Being responsible and accountable allows us to control our own emotions thus offering us the liberty to act in a constructive and healthy manner.

The word responsibility is coined from two words; response and ability. This means that we have an inbuilt ability to choose our responses. In its most basic form, anger is a reactive action happening automatically and often unconsciously. The opposite of such a reaction is responsibility. Responsible behavior results from our own conscious choice. It is based on our goals values and aspirations rather than how we feel at the moment. Being responsible means staying mindful and aware. Responsibility is about understanding the results of our actions now and in the future. It involves doing things and at the same time asking "is the behavior I am engaging in beneficial and desirable in the long run?"

Sometimes, anger seems to be driven by something or someone beyond us. However, it appears so because we are not really aware of the source of these feelings. Basically, anger arises from within and as we get to know more about the emotion, we understand the root cause. Once we understand the mechanism of anger and take a deeper look into ourselves, we realize that the seed of anger was in us long before the circumstance that made us act out. This seed is the real cause of our suffering, not the actual event.

Below are some of the guidelines you can use to become more responsible for your anger and even deal with it.

First, recognize that anger is not the main problem by itself. It is our perception of the particular situation that is the problem. If you assume that a driver cut you off knowingly, then you will get angry. When you look at things more closely, you will realize that the anger was not as a result of the driver; rather it was your perception. Where did the feelings of anger come from? Somewhere inside you. The origin of your anger and reaction is not the other person, it is you. The feeling and the origin are yours.

You are the one who summoned and allowed anger to take control.

Most importantly, try to answer this question; why did you call upon your anger during this situation? Why do you call upon this emotion at certain moments? Anger is a response to something. What are you trying to cover or protect? To answer this question, step into the role of an observer. Look at your situation rationally. Some of the questions you might have to answer are who, what where when and why.

For instance;

Who does this person remind me of?
What felt like it is out of my control at that moment?
When did I feel like this before? Have I been in a similar situation before?
Why did I feel upset in this situation?

Many times when you are feeling out of control, you are recalling something probably from your childhood or earlier times when you did not have any control of the situation. Even though you have become an adult with full control of your choices, thoughts, and feelings, a similar situation might trigger a memory overwhelming you with the vulnerability.

If you have a hard time answering these questions, seek help from a coach or counselor. Once you learn what causes your anger, you will know how to be responsible. Improved responsibility skills will enable you to feel less stressed and even have better relationships. If another person was responsible for your feelings, then there is nothing you could do about it. However, there is some good news. You are responsible for your feelings. And taking responsibility is the only way out.

Secondly, transform your anger.

Anger is a normal part of our emotions and we always carry this fire inside us. We all have the task of guarding our fire so that it does not burn us and our loved ones. It can also be better for us if we can redirect this energy into some positive power. So, instead of being tempered by the fire of anger, we could use it transformatively and constructively as an enlightening force.

Thirdly, know that anger belongs to us.

It does not matter who or what triggered our anger, the emotions is yours and mine. You are the only person responsible for your own emotions and I am the only one controlling my emotions. We are responsible for our own feelings, be they positive or negative. While we can actually blame someone else for the way we feel, it is upon ourselves to manage our feelings and actions.

Fourthly, reduce expectations and catch the anger early on.

Our unfulfilled expectations can lead to anger. When we expect too much from others and ourselves without creating room for failure, it becomes easy to get upset.

Before setting your own standards, make sure that you have the ability to accept results. Be responsible for your expectations and results. Be honest with yourself and acknowledge your abilities. Having expectations is in our human nature but it is up to us to control our attachment to them.

To catch your anger early on, you need to know what it feels like at a low level. Understand your feelings when you are calm. Use the anger diary to study the events that fuel your anger. The sooner you catch that anger, the greater your ability to stay rational and calm the intense feelings. Note that prevention is better than cure.

Fifthly, change your thoughts and inner self.

If anger recedes within us then we should change certain aspects of self to help overcome it. Our thoughts contribute to anger; therefore, we might need to change them. For instance, look for ways to change the absolutism mentality. You are not perfect, you are human.

Finally, adopt some coping strategies and do your betsIf you are challenged by anger, there is a need for you to adjust and improve your coping skills. Anger is very resilient and you might have to do more than you imagined to reach your goals. However, note that you can only do your best to accommodate your needs and goals. Anything beyond your best is outside your power, therefore, you must accept the outcome, no matter what it is. Control what you can and leave the rest to the universe. You do not have to always monitor each aspect of the world. Letting go of the things that are beyond your power is the ultimate freedom. That freedom leads to happiness.

By being responsible for our emotions, more so anger, and aspiring to become better persons, we can transform negative emotions into positive energy and make life more enjoyable. So, be responsible for your anger and use this ability as an antidote for anger.

CHAPTER 9

LONG-TERM AND SHORT-TERM SOLUTION TO ANGER

Although anger can be utterly destructive, it would be weird to live without an emotion that alerts us of wrongdoing. Imagine how the world would be if we did not feel disappointed when things fail to work out the way we expect. What if we did not feel offended when a person wrongs us? It would not feel so good. However, anger is not a ticket to wrong deeds. But, because our lives today are so stressful, anger can get out of control and make us lose focus on what is good. Uncontrolled anger can cost us a lot of things including relationships, jobs and even our own lives.

This realization should not make you angry or fret for that matter because there are some anger management techniques that can help you to mitigate anger in the long term, These techniques can be used to control the potentially destructive emotion more so, for the long term.

First, be aware of the triggers of your anger.

Understanding why you are angry in the first place can help you strategize on getting rid of the emotion. The only time you can understand your anger is when you are not angry. At this juncture, the anger diary comes in handy. Analyze your anger patterns, themes, and triggers after the episode. It is very hard to critically analyze a situation while your mind is still seething with anger. However, for the sake of long term control, it is very important to analyze oneself and the underlying reasons for loss of temper. What causes your anger?

As stated by Socrates, a life without examination is a life not worth living. This also applies to anger management. To understand your anger, recall the last time you were angry and assess all the elements involved in the situation. Answer the following questions;

1. What made you angry?
2. What were the triggers?
3. How did the other people react?
4. How did you react to the reactions of other people?
5. What did you feel after the anger had settled?

Write these answers in a notebook or journal – the more details you can include, the better it is for analysis. Keep recording information from different scenes and compare the details. Gradually, you will identify the similarities and common patterns. After a period of self-analysis, you will be able to master your own emotions.

Secondly, make a choice to not get angry.

ANGER MANAGEMENT

It is said that anger is a choice you do not get angry unless you allow yourself. The main challenge is that we get angry so often that it becomes automatic and losing a temper becomes a normal part of life. Making a choice to not get angry can be hard at first but once you identify your triggers, it becomes easier to control your emotions. Choosing not to get angry requires you to actually know the causes of your upset. Then, identify ways to avoid, control, or ignore them. Note that this second tip will not work well unless you use the first one appropriately.

Did you know that there are some though patterns known to trigger anger? Some thoughts such as "people like that should be prevented from using the road" or 'that is not fair' will only increase the anger. Negative thoughts such as these will keep a person focused on the matter triggering the anger. Once you let these thoughts go, it becomes easier to calm down. Try to avoid absolutism. Phrases such as never (You never pay attention to what I say), always (you always hurt me), should and should not (You should drop me off at work, you should not be with that group), ought or ought not (everyone ought to respect me), must or must not (I must always be neat or I must not burn my food) or, not fair.

Thirdly, mediate

One of the best anger management techniques used in the long term for adults involves meditation. This techniques does not only allow you to have better control of your anger or negative emotion but also can bring about a sense of calm and inner peace. There are a number of meditation techniques you can apply but the most common one for anger management involves chanting some calming phrases such as " I control my mind, I control my anger. I am contented, calm and peaceful. Nothing can pierce the circle of peace protecting me. " Regular practice of this meditation mantra and technique for a few minutes each day will eventually bring a difference in our life.

Fourthly, acknowledge your achievements in controlling anger.

Each time you manage to control your anger or any other negative emotion. Take some time to congratulate yourself and acknowledge your success. Self-recognition has multiple positive effects. The first one is strengthening the urge and ability to control emotions. Moreover, celebrating your own success will have a significant positive effect on your confidence. It will also lower the barriers that hinder your achievements.

Fifthly, look after yourself

Your own practices can either build or jeopardize your health and anger management ability. How much rest do you get? Is your sleep restful or restless? What is your diet and how is your food intake? Lack of rest and the use of alcohol and other substances can make anger management a challenge. Drug abuse lowers inhibitions which are required to stop the body from acting unexpectedly and unacceptably when angry. Watch your own health practices in order to control anger.

ANGER MANAGEMENT

Having control over anger can be very hard especially if losing your temper has become a habit. Anger can become a deeply ingrained practice requiring exceptional efforts to let go. However, with regular application of anger management techniques and perseverance, you will eventually master these negative emotions and enjoy a happier and more productive life.

The above-mentioned techniques are very handy in the long term. However, there are steps you need to take in order to tame your temper in the short term. What can you do when a person or situation is really pushing on your nerves? What can you do when someone cuts you off in traffic and you are fuming? What can you do when a child has refused to cooperate with you? What do you do if the perceptions of other people make your blood pressure to rocket? It is important to deal with anger in a healthy way otherwise it will affect your relationships.

In your moment of anger, think before talking or be completely silent until the emotion has passed. Anger brings about a form of anger which can lead you to say something you will regret later. Take some time to collect your thoughts before voicing them. Allow the other people involved in the situation to think and reconsider the words before stating them. During this moment, take deep breaths, take a walk, and practice the muscle relaxation exercises and any other that might take your mind away from the anger. You need to focus on the matter at hand in a rational way. Anger makes you irrational and you will have a hard time making substantial decisions.

Once you are calm and can think rationally, express your opinion. A clear head will help you look at your perception and the position of the other person. State your opinion in a substantial, assertive and non-confrontational way. The idea is to pass your message without forcing the other person to take a defensive and confrontational position. State your needs and concerns as clearly and directly as possible without trying to control or hurt the others.

When you feel your anger rising, getting some physical exercises can help. First, physical exercises can get your mind off the issue at hand for a while. Run if you can or take a quick walk. Go into a park or follow a nature trail. Spend some time participating in other enjoyable activities. When you come back to the issue that caused your anger, it will be easier to think clearly.

Exercising also involves taking some time out. Breaks are not just for kids in schools. We are all human and sometimes, life presents us with challenges. Give yourself some short breaks whenever thongs get stressful. A few moments of 'me time' can help you to prepare for what is coming ahead without getting irritated or angry.

In some cases, you might not be able to go for a walk or even ignore the matter at hand for a while. In such a situation, you may use a technique such as counting to ten and reciting positive mantras. Counting to ten buys you

ANGER MANAGEMENT

time to cool off and switch from the topic at hand for a while. It turns off the impulse to lash out. Breathe and recite some positive energy mantras such as "I am in control. Nothing will make me lose my temper".

During the break or exercise time, focus on all possible solutions. D not focus so much on what made you mad, rather, assess the situation at hand and select some possible solutions. For instance, if the messy room of your child gets you mad, close the door. If your partner always arrives home late thus delaying dinner time, schedule the meals for later. Regardless of the situation, always remember that anger will not fix anything for you; in fact, it will only make matters worse. Sometimes, the solution to your problem is right in your face. Just shift your attention from that anger to finding a solution for the situation.

One thing that fuels anger intensely is passing the blame to other people. As seen earlier, most of the anger in our lives arise because;

People are rude, inconsistent, and untrustworthy, People do not pay enough attention to the needs of others and they hardly care about you, People expect or demand too much from you, People are mean and cruel. People disrespect, shame and criticize you. They use you or take advantage of your good spirit. People refuse to do their share or responsibility. They also try to manipulate or control you. People are stupid or incompetent, and make you have to wait

ANGER MANAGEMENT

In other words, we always accuse other people thus thinking that we can do nothing about the situation. This criticism or scapegoating only increases the tension within yourself and with other people. Passing the blame only breaks your relationships. One way to control your anger is to avoid pointing fingers at other people and accepting your role in the situation. Use the 'I' statement more often than 'you' statements. For instance, say " I am upset that you did not clear the table after dinner" rather than "you are very self-centered and cannot help with anything in the house." Be respectful and non-confrontational in your arguments. Offer help whenever it is needed.

As seen in a previous topic, grudges are not healthy. They will make you a slave. You will not be able to forgive a person now if you still hold something against them from the past. Forgiveness is a powerful tool and grace is even stronger. If you allow a grudge, anger, and other negative feelings to bring you down and cover your forgiving ability, you can hardly control your anger. You will find yourself wallowing in unwarranted anger, sense of injustice and bitterness if you keep holding grudges.

However, forgiving one wrong strengths your ability to let go of another wrong. Through forgiving, you can learn more from the situation. Forgiveness also strengthens your relationships.

Lightening the mood during that moment of anger can also help you to face the situation and lower your anger. Remember that tip about using your imagination to picture your anger triggering boss as a cartoon? It can be very handy when you are angry. Ty to make every anger triggering situation a lively time – a situation where you can laugh, this way, you release anger faster than you accumulate it. However, humor should not involve sarcasm because it might hurt people's feelings and make things worse.

Use relaxation skills. These breathing and muscle relaxation techniques can be used for both short term and long term anger management. When you feel your anger arising or tempers flaring, apply the relaxation techniques. Take deep breaths, release the tension that is accumulated in different muscles and repeat some meditation phrases such as "I am calm, I will not lose my temper". Relaxation may also involve listening to some calming music as you fill your journal. You may do yoga exercises or whatever it takes to relax.

It is important to acknowledge that controlling anger can be quite the task and some people may find it challenging. If you cannot control your anger, and self-help tools are not helping you, it is okay to seek help from professionals.

CHAPTER 10

PUTTING IT TOGETHER

The use of anger management techniques

In this book, we have described various techniques you can use to manage anger. It may appear as if these techniques have to be practiced in isolation. However, that is not the case. These techniques may be practiced in isolation or in groups. Applying several of them at a go will help you to work on anger from different angles.

When you are facing a situation that might trigger your anger, learn how to stall your reaction. Stop and make some reflections before responding. Below are some steps you may follow.

1. Immediately stop how you are acting and thinking at the first indicator you are getting angry. Using the anger diary, you will be able to know the signs and symptoms that show your anger is rising. Imagery may help you to stop the anger track. Imagine a big red road sign written stop.

2. Practice the deep breathing exercises and repeat the relaxation cues such as saying the words calm and

cool. Use muscle relaxation techniques to reach a calm state.

3. Reflect and try to spot the emotional trigger that is setting you off at that moment. Ask yourself: what thoughts are occupying my head?
What is my body doing?
Am I responding to an incomplete first impression or a real problem?
What do I want from this situation? Is it revenge?
Is it really worth getting angry?
What is likely to happen if I act out?
Is this aggression affecting anyone else?

4. Choose your response wisely. Work to identify an assertive response instead of an aggressive one.

5. Then, after you are sure your response is rational, respond.

> Often, In the middle of an angering situation, chances are, you will feel that things are moving too fast. In fact, you will feel that there is not enough time for you to follow every step of anger management. Still, this is just an illusion. This pressure is only created by the intense feeling of arousal caused by anger. You do not have to respond very fast. Take your time.

If you find that the moment or conversation is getting heated, it is okay to ask for a time out. During the break, go through the anger management steps. Ensure that the way you ask for time out is respectful. For instance, you may say "Kindly allow me to step out for a while. I'll be back in a few minutes to continue without discussion." Time out is a sure way of interrupting the anger process. Therefore, upon returning to the situation, you will be refreshed and better placed to approach it with a new perspective and in an assertive way.

If the situation does not allow you to take a break, try the following steps;

- Be an active listener. When listening to what the other person is saying, do not be quick to state your opinion. Keep your mind open. od not "yes but" them, That is equal to turning the conversation from them to you. That is what you want to avoid. Allow a person to completely share his/her opinion regardless of how much they overstep you.

- Use the 'I' statement to make requests or express your feelings. Basically, a statement such as "you are not caring or understanding" sounds like an accusation. It triggers the defense mechanism of the other person. However, a statement such as "I feel that this situation has brought about a conflict between us" is very positive. It encourages the other person to actually identify the conflict rather than start justifying their position. The goal of communication is to let others know where we stand without belittling or beating them up.

- Make intermittent eye contact. When confronting a person, ensure that you make eye contact. This does not mean staring at the person - it comes off as rude. Intermittent eye contact shows that you are courageous and are willing to defend your stand.

- To create an empathetic mood, try stating the common needs and goals between you and the other person. It can be difficult to identify commonalities between you and a person that is triggering your anger but, that can be beneficial for your relationship.

- Assess whether the person you are talking to has really understood what you were saying. Have you been really heard? If the message is home, continue with the conversation. If you have been misunderstood, re-explain your position. The most important thing is to reduce the chances of a conflict. If the person is too angry to understand, give him/her some time off. Restate your stand using different words. Understand that not everyone has the ability or knowledge to apply the same anger management techniques you are using. If communication becomes impossible at this moment, disengage and continue during another time.

- Refuse to react prematurely. If you need some more time to think things over critically, buy it. Stall the other person until you feel stable in your senses. If you are forced to choose between losing control and walking away, do the latter. It is better to remain in control than to stay angry.

Practice makes perfect

Be sure, you will get a lot of opportunities to practice the anger management skills you have learned. However, you may practice these techniques through role-play exercises. There are some role-playing exercises designed to resemble your anger triggers. You can roleplay on your own or with a partner. First, make a list of those things that trigger your anger. Then, Come up with situations during which you may face these triggers.

If you are role-playing on your own, stand in front of a mirror and assume that someone has angered you. The mirror technique has been used for long by many professional actors therefore; do not feel like you are mad. Standing in front of a mirror allows you to observe your reactions and facial expressions. Recall a time that you were very angry and watch your physical reactions. Now, imagine that a person is standing in front of you and triggering your anger. Picture his/her physical and verbal reactions. Then, say the things you want to tell him/her out loud as if he/she was really there and imagine the reactions. Now, work your anger management techniques into the conversation. You might feel weird or too conscious about your acting at first but gradually, you will pass the initial anxiety and find the exercise very helpful.

If you can access a friend, partner or therapist to practice your skills with, it will be much better. Basically, it is easier to get into the role when you have an actual person to practice with. First, explain to your partner what you want then describe a scene that triggers your anger. Let the partner act as you respond. Ensure that you are incorporating your anger management skills in the role.

Programs

Some people will learn how to control their anger by themselves. You might find that after putting the techniques learned in this book to practice, it is easy to manage your anger. However, some people will not be as successful. In this case, it is advisable that one considers other types of anger management programs such as individual and group therapy.

For some people, the best and easiest way of changing their inappropriate anger management practices is through a psychologist. Some people have to work with licensed mental health practitioners on an individual basis or in a group setting. A therapist who has an unbiased opinion can help you deal with anger. If you opt for group therapy, it is even more advantageous because other members of the group will share their opinions and experiences. An anger management therapist will also be knowledgeable in the kind of anger management strategies you need to apply more in your life. He/she will help you to personalize a set of anger management techniques for changing your behavior and thinking.

If you choose to use the therapy route, ensure that you select the right the correct kind of therapist. In this world, there are multiple practices of therapy and a large number of therapists subscribing to different schools of thoughts. There are therapists applying psychodynamics, dynamics, psychospiritual and humanistic schools of thought. All of them are good and they help you to get in touch with your emotions and feelings in a deeper way. However, in anger management, what you want to learn is control of emotions. Instead of exploring anger, the person seeking anger management assistance looks for ways to control how they react. Putting this into consideration, a cognitive behavioral therapist is generally the best option for anger management.

There are other characteristics you will want to look for while selecting a therapist. First, any therapist you choose should be licensed. That will depend on the state or country you are in. secondly, you will want to inquire if the therapist is actually trained in anger management therapies and techniques. Has this therapist specialized in anger management therapy or is he/she trying out with you?

A typical anger management therapy course will unfold less like a traditional therapy session and more like a class. You will learn how to become conscious of your emotions, physical and cognitive responses to anger, and the different ways to respond to conflicts and triggers. Depending on your personal anger challenges and needs, the therapist will help you work on breathing exercises, muscle relaxation techniques, safe mechanisms of releasing anger, physically, emotionally and mentally, communication skills and cognitive restructuring. Basically, cognitive restructuring involves disputing and changing your thought patterns and consequently reshaping your emotions.

Normally, the success and effectiveness of therapy is majorly determined by your own dedication and hard work. How badly do you want to take control of your emotions? How regularly do you attend the sessions? How often do you practice your homework? On average, the effects of this therapy are visible after eight or ten sessions.

Anger management classes

Some organizations may offer anger management classes through the employee benefit plan. There are other organizations dedicated to serving the community and may offer such therapy sessions. Anger management classes have a different quality and length depending on the provider. While some sessions may span for weeks or even months, others are only designed to last one or two weekends. It is better to choose a longer class because you will be exposed to more information and have ample time to practice. However, if you do not have enough time to attend a length therapy session, settle for a short one. Regardless of the length of therapy sessions, you will have assignments to complete, projects and quizzes to track your progress.

Before settling for a class, think about your needs. What are you dealing with? What would you like to achieve? Do you need general anger management help or does your problem fit more in couple's therapy? Is it your workplace or work colleagues that trigger your anger? If so, would you rather attend classes provided by your organization?

If you have been mandated by the court or asked by your employer to get anger management help, you have to choose an approved therapist or class that will help you keep track of the progress and give you a formal proof showing that you participated in and completed the sessions.

Handling a relapse

As you work towards gaining full control of your emotions, you might encounter moments when you relapse to your old habits. There is no guarantee that these techniques will work within the first attempt. Sometimes you will find yourself becoming aggressive, inappropriately angry and even belligerent. Regardless of the intensity of a relapse, the biggest favor you can do for yourself is refusing to give up. Do not let all you learned to go to waste just because of a setback.

Do not allow a lapse to turn into a scapegoat for quitting, let that relapse be your stronger comeback. Do not forego all your gains just because of a fail. Let it be a learning experience. Assess the lapse and learn how it occurred. Which part of your anger management plan was insufficient? How can you prevent another lapse from occurring? Use the information to improve your anger management program, to work better next time.

For example, if you face one of the anger triggers, and your strategy for dealing with that trigger did not work, write that down next, consider what you could have done differently to handle that situation without blowing up. If it was a new thing that made you relapse, note it down and identify a plan for dealing with it. Think things out in advance and anticipate any causes of relapses. Remember that – you have more to lose by giving up and more to gain by holding on to that program. Do not give up.

ANGER MANAGEMENT

CONCLUSION

Thank you for making it through to the end of *Anger Management: A Step-by-Step Guide to Overcoming Your Anger & Emotion*. Let us hope it was informative and has provided you with the tools you need to manage anger and other emotions. Please note that it may take a while before you notice the effects of applying these anger management techniques. However, every step you take towards becoming better at anger management will redefine you, your relationships and your whole life. There will be anger outbursts and maybe some relapses making you feel lost and lonely for a while. However, do not give up. You are on a worthy course and the freedom you will get from better anger management is worth fighting for. Furthermore, there will be plenty of room for rediscovering and growth with the right guidance and steps.

The anger will not always feel stronger than you. This journey is full of ups and downs. Some days you will feel weak while others you will be as strong as ever. This alteration of moods is okay because you are still learning - Discovering things about yourself which you had buried for so long.

The moment you understand the anger, it becomes easier to manage. Anger management is important in our everyday life. This book has taken you through anger management techniques. There is no one specific thing that a person can do to manage anger overnight. However,

ANGER MANAGEMENT

if you follow management steps with dedication and full commitment, you will reach your goals. Combine a number of treatment options if they will help you reach your goals. When working with a therapist, ensure that you follow all the instructions given and keep an open communication channel.

The next step is to stop reading and start applying the lessons in real life. Do whatever you have identified as necessary to curb anger and ensure the health and wellness of you and the people around you. You will find that many people are still ignorant about the proper ways of anger management. You will also realize that the majority of those people who seem to have full control are just suppressing anger, and it might harm them one day. You could try to engage them and share a thing or two you have learned herein. Feel free to recommend/gift this book to them.

You might also need to refer to this book at a later date. The information shared can be used at any time any day. Keep it and review it as often as you want. Just because you have reached the end of the book does not mean that there is nothing else to learn about anger and you. Read more and expand your horizons. It is the only way you will gain the control you seek. Pay attention to the changes that will flood your life as soon as you start managing your anger, more so assertively. Use some of the tips herein to make the world a better place.

www.ingramcontent.com/pod-product-compliance
Lightning Source LLC
Chambersburg PA
CBHW052100110526
44591CB00013B/2291